Get Around

in Greece

The all-in-one travel and language guide

Antigone Veltsidou Bentham
Clive Aldiss with Youla Notia and
Matthew Hancock

PASSPORT BOOKS
NTC/Contemporary Publishing Company

Library of Congress Cataloging-in-Publication Data
is available from the United States Library of Congress

Photographs
All photographs by Steve Parker, except the following:

Cover photograph © Phyllis Picardi/Photo Network
A.G.E. Fotostock: back cover (bm)
Anthony Blake: p68, 76(b), 77, 80(t), 82, 83, 86, 87
Cephas: p76(t), 78(b), 81, 84(b), 85, 89
Getty Images: back cover (t), p5(b), 16(b), 17, 18, 19, 21, 95
The Image Bank: p2(b), 3(m), 9, 10, 11, 12, 15, 24, 39(br), 49(br), 52(br), 54(br), 55(bl), 59(m), 63, 69(ml), 102
Life File: p1, 2(t), 3(t), 4, 5(t), 8, 13(m), 14, 16(t), 26, 42(m), 96
Pictor International – London: spine, back cover (br), p6(t), 13(b), 20, 27, 91(b)
Zefa Pictures: p22, 23, 25

Map: Malcolm Porter

This edition published by Passport Books
An imprint of NTC/Contemporary Publishing Company
4255 West Touhy Avenue
Lincolnwood (Chicago), Illinois 60646-1975 U.S.A.

Published in cooperation with BBC Worldwide. "BBC" and the
BBC logotype are trademarks of the British Broadcasting Corporation
and are used under license.
© BBC Worldwide Ltd 1998.
All rights reserved. No part of this book may be reproduced,
stored in a retrieval system, or transmitted in any form
or by any means, electronic, mechanical, photocopying,
recording, or otherwise, without the prior permission of
NTC/Contemporary Publishing Company.

Printed in the United Kingdom

International Standard Book Number: 0-8442-0155-3 book
International Standard Book Number: 0-8442-0188-X package
1 3 5 7 9 11 12 10 8 6 4 2

Insider's guide to Greece | page 1
Introduction
Athens, The Cyclades, Crete, the Dodecanese Islands, the Peloponnese, the Ionian Islands, Central Mainland Greece and the Sporades, Thessaloniki, Northern Mainland Greece and the North and North Eastern Aegean
Holidays, festivals and events

Bare necessities | page 28
Essential words and phrases
Numbers, times, days of the week

Getting around | page 36,
Traveling around Greece: car rental and public transportation

Somewhere to stay | page 48
Finding accommodations: hotels, rentals, campsites

Buying things | page 58
Food, clothes, stamps

Café life | page 70
Getting drinks and snacks

Eating out | page 76
Ordering a meal

Menu reader | page 84
Understanding Greek menus

Entertainment and leisure | page 90
Finding events, getting tickets and information

Emergencies | page 98
Doctors, dentists, pharmacies, car breakdown, theft

Language builder | page 109
The basics of Greek grammar

Answers | page 113
Key to Language works and Try it out

Dictionary | page 115
Full list of Greek words with English translations

Sounds Greek | inside cover
Simple guide to pronouncing Greek

INTRODUCTION

Get Around in Greece will enable you to pick up the language, travel with confidence and experience the very best the country has to offer. You can use it both *before* a trip, to pick up the basics of the language and to plan your itinerary, and *during* your trip, as a phrasebook and as a source of practical information in all the key travel situations.

Contents
Insider's guide to Greece An introduction to the country, a guide to Athens, and region-by-region highlights for planning itineraries.
Bare necessities The absolute essentials of Greek.
Seven main chapters covering key travel situations from *Getting around* to *Entertainment and leisure*. Each chapter has three main sections: *information* to help you understand the local way of doing things; *Phrasemaker*, a phrasebook of key words and phrases; *Language works/Try it out*, simple dialogues and activities to help you remember the language.
Menu reader A key to menus in Greek.
Language builder A simple introduction to Greek grammar.
1000-word dictionary The most important Greek words you will come across with their English translations.
Sounds Greek A clear guide to pronouncing the language and the Greek alphabet.

How to use the book
Before you go You can use the *Insider's guide* to get a flavor of the country and plan where you want to go. To pick up the language, the *Phrasemaker* sections give you the key words and phrases; the *Language works* dialogues show the language in action, and *Try it out* offers you a chance to practice for yourself.

During your trip The *Insider's guide* offers tips on the best things to see and do in the main cities. The *Phrasemaker* works as a phrasebook with all the key language to help you get what you want. Within each chapter there is also practical "survival" information to help you get around and understand the country.

Insider's guide to Greece

Greece's historical setting

Greece's history begins some 5,000 years ago, with an early Cycladic culture. The latter stage of this era saw the first Minoan palaces in Crete, at Knossos and Phaestos (see p11). The Minoan civilization was an advanced one, with a trade of both artifacts and ideas, and remarkable naturalistic art and sculpture. Around the same time, the Mycenaean civilization – centered on Mycenae (modern Mikines) in the Peloponnese – was flourishing. Much influenced by the Minoans, the Mycenaeans enjoyed an affluent lifestyle evident from bronze, silver and gold articles found there (see p14).

Cape Sounion

Following the collapse of the Mycenean civilization in around 1200 BC, the Greek city states emerged and Greek colonies were established overseas. Much of our knowledge of this time stems from Homer's works, the Iliad and the Odyssey.

In the fifth century BC, Athens became the cultural, commercial and political center of the world. Despite the wars between the various city states, there was a flowering of achievement in philosophy, art, science, literature and drama. The Parthenon (the Doric temple on the Acropolis) was built under Pericles and dedicated to the Goddess Athena. This century also saw the Peloponnesian war between the great rivals, Athens and Sparta. Although Athens had great power and a maritime empire, the Spartans emerged supreme and

INSIDER'S GUIDE TO GREECE

remained so until defeated by Thebes in 371 BC.

Philip of Macedon defeated Athens and Thebes in 338 BC, making Macedonia the leading power in Greece. His son, Alexander the Great, ruled an empire that reached as far as India. Following Alexander's death, the Greek city states tried to reassert their independence. Finally, the last Macedonian War led to Rome colonizing Greece: Hellenism became a major influence on Rome.

With the collapse of the Roman Empire, Greece became a province of the Byzantine (Eastern Roman) Empire and by 1460 control had passed to the Ottoman Turks. With only a brief respite under the Venetians (1686–1715), the Greeks remained under the absolute domination of the Turks until 1829 with the Greek War of Independence.

Greece then became a monarchy, with first a Bavarian and then a Danish King. As Turkey retained control of some Greek territory, conflict between the countries continued, with Cyprus still under dispute today.

During the Second World War, the country was occupied by the Nazis from 1941 to 1944, a time which brought great hardship, especially to Crete and Athens. Following the war, the pro-communist guerrilla army (ELAS) was prevented from seizing power by American and British intervention. The ensuing Greek Civil War lasted until 1949, when ELAS was finally broken, and the country left shattered.

A monarchy was installed once more, but deposed in a military coup in 1967. Military rule lasted until the students' uprising at the Athens Polytechnic and the invasion of Cyprus by Turkey in 1974. The monarchy was finally abolished and democracy restored.

Greece became a full member of the European Community in 1981, but being an essentially rural country geographically remote from the rest of the EC, it has remained one of the EC's poorest members, heavily dependent on tourism.

The people, geography and climate

The Greeks are immensely proud of their country and culture and most will go out of their way to make sure visitors fully appreciate it. In rural areas in particular, you can expect the friendliest of welcomes, though tourists are too numerous to be treated as special in some of the busier spots. Though essentially laid back, the Greeks like nothing better than having a good debate, so it may sound as if they are arguing even when they are not! Religion is an important part of Greek culture, and many Greeks take their Orthodox faith very seriously.

INSIDER'S GUIDE TO GREECE

Greece is famous for its islands, of which there are literally thousands, all with their own character. As a rule, those north of Athens are far greener and lusher, but all islands have their own distinct qualities of space and a special light which gives colors a unique brightness. Greece also has a mainland often overlooked by visitors, yet with a wealth to offer from tremendous archaeological sites to dramatic mountain terrain, from the remote, wooded slopes of the north to the craggy peaks of the Peloponnese.

Predominantly Mediterranean, Greece has hot summers and relatively mild winters, except in the

the Acropolis, Athens

mountain regions, and is justly famous for its sunshine, around 3,000 hours of it per year. The seasons can change abruptly. Generally, April to June are the best times to visit the southern islands and the Peloponnese. In April, areas which become parched and barren in high summer are green and pleasant, although the sea has only just begun to warm up. September and October are also good times, though by October the sun sets at around six o'clock. The sea is at its warmest from July to September, when the north of Greece is pleasantly hot, while in the south, swimming remains comfortable into early November. If you are contemplating a visit between December and March, remember it can be wet and gets very cold, especially in the north and the mountains where snow falls annually.

Currency and changing money

The Greek currency is the drachma. It is written **δραχμή**, plural **δραχμές (δρχ** or **Δρχ)** Greece is basically a cash economy and most Greeks use neither checks nor credit cards. Most hotels, large shops and department stores in central and main tourist areas will accept credit cards, most usually Visa. Bear in mind, however, that you may get a discount if you pay

Santorini, the Cyclades

cash. There are automatic currency conversion points available at some central locations, such as Syntagma Square in Athens and the airports, and the National Bank of Greece has now installed automatic teller machines at nearly all branches. They also take Visa and function in a number of languages. Traveler's checks are widely exchangeable, except in the most remote locations, where it is best to take sufficient cash with you. Banks generally open 8 am–2 pm from Monday to Friday; you can also change money in hotels or travel agencies, but beware of high commission rates in hotels.

Visa and entry requirements

Travelers with United States, Canadian, South African, Australian and New Zealand passports do not need visas and are entitled to stay in Greece as tourists for up to 90 days. Greece is a full European Community member and entry formalities for EC citizens are minimal. Other nationalities should consult their local Greek embassy or consulate.

For addresses of embassies and consulates in Greece, see p99.

Special needs travelers

Though Greece does not have a huge range of facilities for those with special needs, the EOT (the national tourist authority) can supply details of travel companies that specialize in vacations for the disabled and a list of suitably equipped hotels.

A note on spellings of Greek place names

There is no single way of writing Greek names in English and various transliterations exist to show Greek pronunciation. On road signs you may see Piraeus, Piraeas, even Pireefs. In this book, established English transliteration for classical places is given along with the modern Greek pronunciation, eg Mycenae (Mikines). For other places, the closest transliteration of modern Greek is used, eg Idra (Hydra).

Samaria Gorge, Crete

Athens

*D*espite its evocative history and dramatic setting, modern Athens is not immediately appealing, a sprawling mass of uniform concrete buildings constructed to withstand earthquakes. Indeed, the city's midsummer heat and frequent pollution problems can leave anything but a positive impression. Nevertheless, visitors who take the time to see more than the Acropolis get to know a different city, one with quieter backstreets resonant with the sound of caged birds, leading to leafy squares sheltering shady cafés. Most tourists stay around the attractive Plaka, an area of 19th-century houses curling around the slopes of the Acropolis, its stepped streets full of tavernas and shops. The Plaka forms part of a largely pedestrianized area stretching to Athens' main shopping streets and atmospheric main market, while most of the city's main sights are within walking distance of the central Syntagma Square. But above all else it is the Athenians themselves who make the city, one which remains one of the safest and liveliest in Europe; an outdoor capital whose bars, clubs, tavernas, and streets come alive after dark.

Don't miss

Tha Acropolis Situated on a hill topped by the ruins of the Parthenon, the Acropolis symbolizes not only ancient Greece, but the dawning of Western civilization. The Parthenon itself is a clever optical illusion: its columns seem taller, lighter and more tapered than they really are. Two and a half millennia of invasions and pollution have exacted a heavy toll, but this is justifiably the site which most visitors head for first. Preferably see it around dawn, sunset, or by full moon, and check the opening hours (tel: 323 6665)
A stroll around the Plaka, for a taste of a village within a city; head for the atmospheric Plateia Avissinias behind Monastiráki. See the Agora, the city's ancient

INSIDER'S GUIDE TO GREECE

the Acropolis

marketplace, and the Stoa of Attalos, once a commercial arcade and now a museum.

The main market, off the pedestrianized streets north of the Plaka on Athinás, an atmospheric 19th-century covered area full of every food item imaginable; look out for the flower market nearby on Eólu, next to the Ayía Iríni church.

A trip up Lykavitos, the highest hill in the city, affording superb views over the Acropolis and the city from its summit. Go up on the funicular (teleferík) from Aristippou Street, and walk down its leafy paths for a drink in fashionable Kolonaki Square.

Temple of Olympian Zeus

A visit to the Museum of Cycladic and Ancient Art, a small museum in Kolonaki with an exquisite and unrivaled collection of third millennium BC Cycladic idols.

The Monastiráki flea market, especially on a Sunday – highly atmospheric, very crowded and occasionally the source of a real bargain.

The National Archaeological Museum, to the north of Athens' center in Patission Street; highlights are the frescoes from Santoríni (or Thíra), the gold relics in the Mycenaean Hall and the classical Statue of Poseidon.

A picnic on Filopáppou Hill Walk through the backstreets of the pleasant area of Thisseion. Go uphill to the prominent Filopáppou Monument, for some of the best views of the Acropolis and the Roman amphitheater, the Odeion of Herodes Atticus.

A wander around the National Gardens, once the palace gardens; a cool respite from Athens' traffic.

A trip to the Temple of Olympian Zeus, perhaps the most impressive Roman relic and once the largest temple in Greece, with imposing Corinthian columns, some standing, some toppled. It is situated by Hadrian's Arch, once the edge of the classical city.

A night out in Exarchia, one of the liveliest areas in Athens and home to countless tavernas and ouzeris.

Clubs and bars

Avant Garde Boulevard, in Vouliagmenis Avenue, one of the city's most happening clubs.

Camel Club, in Glyfada. A huge club which holds 3,000–3,500 people. Atmosphere is guaranteed, especially after 1am, when the Greek music gets going.

Latin, Exarchia, for live music, from Greek to jazz or folk.

Memphis Booze, behind the Hilton hotel, for alternative rock.

Rembétiki Istoriá, in Exarchia, for genuine 1930s Athenian music.

ATHENS

Romeo, in Glyfada, a great place to catch Greek bouzoúki music, and an all nighters' favorite.
Taksími, Exarchia, another place to catch rembétika folk music in an old neoclassical building.

Coffee and pastry in

Fílion, Kolonaki; take a seat, have a coffee and watch the rich and beautiful walk by on this fashionable square.
De Profúndis, Plaka, with 50 kinds of tea, plus great cakes.
To Trístrato, just off Plateia Filomoussou Eterias, serving delicious coffee and sweets.
Zónar's, in Panepistimiou Street. An old aristocratic café which retains much of the charm that has inspired writers in the past.

A meal or ouzo in

Apótsos, in Panepistimiou Street, the oldest ouzeri in Athens, plastered with hundreds of dated advertisements, with an unforgettable atmosphere; only open at lunchtimes.
Cotton Club, a surprisingly reasonable bar-restaurant in Syntagma Square, frequented by business executives, journalists and politicians.
Eden, Plaka. Set in an old mansion, this is the city's most established vegetarian restaurant, with a wide variety of dishes and very good red wine from the barrel.
Gerofínikas, near Kolonaki, an inexpensive place with Greek and oriental dishes.
Ideal, in Panepistimiou St, art-nouveau and high-qua place in the heart of the city.
Kioúpia, Glyfada. Fairly expensive but with a large range of traditional recipes from all over Greece.
Kírios Píl-Poúl, in the Thisseion area. One of the most creative (and expensive) restaurants in town with great views of the Acropolis.
Rozalía, off Exarchia Square, an excellent inexpensive taverna with a

Lykavitos

leafy garden in summer and a good choice of dishes.
Scholarkío, a traditional ouzeri-cum-taverna in a balconied wooden building in the Plaka.

Transportation

Most areas of interest can be reached on foot, but for some sites you may need to take public transportation. This is inexpensive, though it can be slow and crowded.

Temple of Poseidon

Trolley buses
The distinctive buff-yellow trolley buses – surviving imported relics from the old Soviet Union – provide the simplest method of getting around the city center. Routes 7 and 8 follow a circular route; 7 passes the National Gardens to the National Archaeological Museum and back into Vassilissis Sofias. Route 8 takes basically the same route in a counterclockwise direction.

Buses
Bus route information is clearly displayed at main stops. Buses are a useful way to reach the suburbs.

Tickets
Tickets are valid for all buses including trolley buses and are inexpensive, with a flat fare for the whole of Greater Athens. They are available at the street booths found throughout the city, as well as at the plastic bus and trolley company booths at bus terminals. Tickets are valid for one trip and must be bought before getting on, and then cancelled on board in the orange machines near the doors. A monthly pass is also available.

Taxis
These are reasonably priced compared to most European cities, and a yellow cab ride can be an adventure in itself. Hailing one needs determination and speed; once inside do not expect to be the only passenger, as cabs can be shared. Ensure the driver has turned the meter on and that the Tariff is on number one, unless it's after midnight (when Tariff two means the price is doubled). You pay extra for being picked up at the airport, a port or railway station and for luggage.

The Subway
The Athens subway *(electrikó)* has a number of useful stops. Subway tickets cost the same as for the buses and trolleys; buy your ticket at the station – from a ticket booth or machine – and cancel it in the orange machines as you go onto the platform.

Useful subway stops:
Piraeus for the main harbor for boats to the islands, a 30-minute trip from central Athens.
Thisseion for Filopappou hill and the Agora.
Monastiráki for the Acropolis, the Plaka and the flea market.
Omónia for the National Archaeological Museum and

ATHENS

Exarchia (both are some ten minutes' walk).

Day trips from Athens

Piraeus
Take the subway to Piraeus and visit the harbor of Mikrolímano (or Turkolímano), to enjoy a fish lunch, perhaps after a visit to the Sunday flea market near the main harbor. The Archaeological museum is worth a look, too: don't miss the life-size bronze statue dedicated to Apollo.

Sóunion
This ancient temple, on Attiki's most southerly tip, is the perfect place to watch the sun go down. It can be reached on the orange Attiki bus from Plateía Aigíptou.

Kessarianí Monastery
An eleventh-century monastery is to be found in a beautiful shady grove of cypress and pine trees, on the western flank of fabled Mount Immitós; it is most easily reached by car or by taxi.

Skiniás Beach
Beyond historic Marathóna (Marathon) and its lake, Skiniás is a long, pine-backed, curving stretch of sand, with shallow sea (good for children), a fine view south and plenty of tavernas among the pines. It is about 90 minutes by car (or by bus from Plateía Aigíptou).

Mount Párnitha (Parnes)
Drive to the Párnitha *teleferík* cable car which whisks you up to the summit. There are amazing views of Athens and beyond, with refreshing cool air and some fine country walks. There is also a casino, a crumbling hotel, a nature reserve and a weekend refuge for climbers and walkers, serving food and drink.

Saronic Gulf Islands
Join the Athenians who use these nearby islands as a fresh and tempting escape when the pace and heat get too much in the capital. They can all be reached in 1–3 hours by the fast Flying Dolphin hydrofoils from Piraeus (for Aegina) or Zéa Marina (for Póros, Idra and Spetses), or even on a one-day cruise from Paleó Fáliron east of Piraeus.

■ Aegina: Highlights are the Temple of Aphaea – a truly idyllic location above the artificiality of

Póros

Ayía Marina down the hillside – and an ouzo with *mezé* on the waterfront in Aegina harbor.

■ Póros: Try catching a motorboat across to the beach below the Monastery of Zodóchos Pigís or go up into the hills to the lovely setting of the Temple of Poseidon, perfect in spring. A stone's throw away from Póros is the Peloponnese; take a water taxi across to Galatás and walk southeast to the lemon groves.

■ Idra (Hydra): This fashionable island has one of the most picturesque harbors in the Aegean. What it lacks in beaches it makes up for in style.

■ Agístri: This pretty and tiny island is the least frequented of the group and so the least developed. Simply swim, stroll or relax here.

The Cyclades

Santorini

Perhaps the best-known group of islands, the Cyclades provide the archetypal image of winding, whitewashed Greek villages, most typified by Mykonos and Santoríni, the most frequented and cosmopolitan islands of the group.

Don't miss

Santoríni (or Thira)
The sheer cliffs of this volcanic island rising above the sea are one of the greatest sights, not only in Greece but in the whole Mediterranean. Don't miss the clifftop town of Ia or the weird black sand beaches on its flatter eastern side; take a trip to the volcanic islet *(caldéra)* of Thirassiá.

Mykonos
This island is famous for its nightlife and cosmopolitan visitors, attracted by its idyllic main town and superb beaches. It is also within easy reach of the temples and site of ancient Délos, the neighboring island that was the birthplace of the legendary twins Artemis and Apollo.

Ios
Ios town is basically one huge nightclub that is quiet only in the morning, when visiting youth sleeps off the night before on the fine beaches such as Milopótas and Magganári.

Páros and Náxos
In the center of the group, these islands offer contrasting landscapes, although both have some wonderful beaches. Náxos is hillier – rising to over 3,500 feet – and its main charm lies in the quiet countryside interior villages with their Venetian influence. Páros has a lively nightlife in the capital Parikiá and offers a variety of inland and coastal scenery, including the pretty islet Andíparos.

Sérifos and Sífnos
These quieter islands can be combined as they lie on the same main boat route. Sérifos has one of the most beautiful capitals in the country, rising high above its surroundings with wonderful views out to sea. Sífnos has a pleasant variety of villages, walks, sandy beaches such as Vathí, and sights including the photogenic seaside monastery of Chrissopigí.

Tínos and Andros
Tínos is a conservative island with traditional inland villages such as Falatádo. The island is known as a quiet religious center based around its shrine of Panayía Evangelístria, though it comes alive during the pilgrimages of March and August (see p26–27). Andros is another quiet option, mainly geared to Athenian weekenders, though its main resort, Bátsi, is lively. Its attractive inland villages and countryside are at their best in spring.

Kéa (or Tziá)
The nearest Cycladic island to the mainland remains among the least visited by tourists, perhaps as the main link is by boat from Lávrion, not Piraeus. However, it is justifiably popular with Athenians and the capital, Ioulís (or Kéa), is a treat.

Crete (Kríti)

This southernmost, mountainous island is large enough to feel like a separate country and offers a range of attractions at all times of the year.

Haniá

Don't miss

- Visit Knossós (near Iráklion). This Minoan palace was the place where, according to legend, the Minotaur was confined until Theseus arrived to slay the beast. The palace, which was only excavated at the beginning of the century, is now a vivid reconstruction of the how it was 3,500 years ago.
- Visit the other Minoan sites at Phaestós, about an hour to the south in a magnificent setting, and the tranquil Palace of Mália, east of Iráklion.
- Explore the Archaeological Museum of Iráklion. This veritable treasure trove contains finds from the above-mentioned sites and elsewhere in Crete. Don't miss the frescoes and jewelry or the miniature Minoan sculptures.
- Visit the attractive Venetian harbor towns of Réthymnon and Haniá, the former with its own beach and the latter with a fine market.
- Walk down the beautiful Samariá Gorge, Europe's longest, a challenging (but extremely popular) five-hour walk downhill to the sea, best done as part of a circular trip by bus from Haniá. With your own transportation, an alternative is the Imbros ravine, a three-hour walk down a parallel gorge; it is shorter and marginally less spectacular, but far more solitary.
- Stay in a mountain village such as Ayíos Yióryios on the plains of Lasíthi, Crete's rural heartland and home to traditional white-sailed grain windmills. In springtime, the mountains are filled with flowers and ideal for walking.
- Seek out one of Crete's quieter coastal hideaways, such as Loutró on the south coast, accessible only by boat, or the palm beaches of Vái or Itanos in the far east.

Phaestós

The Dodecanese (Dodekánissa)

Dodekánissa means the "twelve islands," though there are in fact 14 inhabited islands in this fairly diverse group. For true isolation, Kastellórizo, with its attractive main town, is some 320 nautical miles from Piraeus but, like other islands in the group, seemingly just a swim away from Turkey. Dating from medieval times, the Crusaders' castles remain a dominant and unifying feature of the Dodecanese, along with the signs of subsequent Turkish and Italian occupations (the Dodecanese were returned to Greece only in 1948). There are the remnants of mosques in Rhodes and Kos and Italian architecture is apparent from the interwar years.

harbor, Rhodes town

Don't miss

Rhodes (Ródos)
The largest and most popular of the group, Rhodes is highly developed between the airport and Rhodes town. However, go in its mild springs and autumns, when a stroll round Rhodes' handsome walled town is a must.

■ See the mosaics and ornate interior of the Palace of the Grand Masters in Rhodes town, built by the Knights of St. John, and the imposing Knights Hospital containing the Archaeological Museum. Have a stroll down the medieval Street of the Knights.
■ Visit the handsome harbor, Mandráki, with its fort and old windmills.
■ Stay in the walled town of Líndos, dominated by its ancient acropolis. A walk to the top is worthwhile to see the restored Temple of Lindian Athena. The little harbor below the acropolis, Saint Paul, is where the saint landed on the island.
■ Swim on the beaches on the east coast such as Haráki.
■ Visit the lush inland butterfly valley, Petaloúdhes, the breeding ground of tiger moths.

THE DODECANESE (DODEKÁNISSA)

- See the ruins of ancient Kámiros, a ruined Doric city in a beautiful setting.
- Take a day trip to the nearby, sparsely populated island of Hálki, with its restored village of Emborió; or the lush and remote Tílos, dotted with the remains of castles. Or stay on rocky Symi with its precipitous neoclassical harbor and delightfully quiet upper town, Ano Symi.
- Go to the pretty inland village of Píli with its ruined castle.
- Take a trip to Kalymnos, a mountainous but hospitable island once famous for its sponge fishing.
- Visit the nearby volcanic island of Níssyros, a green island with an attractive port, Mandráki. Don't miss a trip down into the smoldering volcano, an unforgettable experience.

Acropolis, Lindos, Rhodes

Kárpathos
This remote and mountainous island is hard to get to and tricky to travel around, and so remains relatively unspoiled. Don't miss Olimbos, a mountain village where women still wear traditional dress, or the wonderful beaches at Ayíos Nikólaos, Finíki and the capital, Pigádhia.

Kos
One of the Dodecanese's most visited islands. The capital, Kos, is lively in summer and retains an oriental feel with its minarets and palm trees.
- See the Asklepion, built in the 4th century BC as a temple and infirmary, which used the medicinal knowledge of Hippocrates, who was born on Kos. There are fine views from the top.
- Visit the island's beaches such as Kefalos for great swimming.

Léros
This little-visited but dramatic island of hills and wooded slopes has the attractive Neoclassical main town of Ayía Marína, well positioned near the sea and overlooked by a castle.

Pátmos
The holy island of Pátmos, sometimes described as the "Jerusalem of the Aegean" is one of the jewels of the Dodecanese. It was here in a cave that Saint John wrote the *Apocalypse*. The island's main attraction is the fine Chóra, surrounded by medieval ramparts.
- See the monastery of Saint John with its array of religious displays.
- Go to the lovely beaches such as Kámbos and Psilí Ammos, best reached by walking down the island's attractive network of paths.
- Take a day trip to the island of Lípsi, with a lovely harbor and sandy coves.

Palace of the Grand Masters, Rhodes

13

The Peloponnese (Pelopónnisos)

This rugged peninsula stretches to the south of mainland Greece and is technically an island, split off by the Corinth canal, the crossing of which is an experience in itself. This large, mountainous area has a wealth of ancient and Byzantine sites and some fine beaches. If you want to see snowcapped mountains, the birthplace of the Olympic games, and a superb golden beach all within a few hours, this could be the place for you.

Epidaurus

Don't miss

Epidaurus (Epídavros)
Site of the superbly preserved ancient theater, this is a must. In summer, catch the classical plays performed here for their atmosphere (even if you cannot understand the ancient Greek).

Náfplion
On the Gulf of Argolis, this is one of the finest Greek provincial towns. It is dominated by the Venetian fort of Palamídi, over 650 feet above the town. The climb up is worth it for the view, but for the less energetic, the fort's rear gate can be reached by road.

Mycenae (Mikínes)
In ancient times, this city was known for its wealth and as the capital of Agamemnon. You can see the old Citadel, reached via the famous Lion Gate, and the Mycenaean Beehive Tombs, named because of their conical shape, said to be up to 3,500 years old.

Arcadía
A beautiful and lush mountainous area which is ideal for those seeking traditional Greece, as exemplified in the mountain villages of Dimitsána and Vitína.

THE PELOPONNESE (PELOPÓNNISOS)

Monemvasía
This is an atmospheric walled Byzantine city hidden behind a vast rock. Wander around its alleyways, ancient houses and churches, and clamber up to the upper town for fantastic views over the sea.

The Máni and the south
A wild area south of Kalamáta, the Máni is characterized by its unique tower houses in villages such as Arópoli and Váthia (see p48). Don't miss the amazing underground caves at Pirgos Dhirou, or the fine beach resorts of Stoúpa and Ayíos Nikólaos. Visit the nearby atmospheric harbor town of Gítheion, the departure point for the mountainous island of Kíthira with its fine Chóra, a perfect summer getaway.

Mystras
This is an uninhabited Byzantine town near the modern city of Sparta (Spárti). The whole site – with its palace, castle and beautiful complex of churches and monasteries – clings to the lush lower slopes of Mount Taígetus.

Pílos and the west
Pílos is an atmospheric town set on a spectacular harbor and guarded by two medieval castles, from where you can visit the superb ancient remains of Nestor's Palace. Go to the western Peloponnese's sweeping beaches such as at Koróni.

Olympía
This is the site that gave birth to and hosted the Olympic Games for around a millennium. The flame of the modern games is still lit here. The highlight is the remains of the stadium itself.

Great train rides
Don't miss a ride on the train from Diakoftó, on the north coast, up into the mountains as far as Kalávrita. This wonderful journey converts partway into a rack-and-pinion mountain affair. Another great train ride is between Argos and Trípolis, a slow ride with superb scenery.

Monemvasía

The Ionian Islands

olive grove, Corfu

Lying just to the west of mainland Greece, the Ionian Islands all show some legacy of Venetian times and not only are but feel close to Europe. Unlike the Cyclades, these islands are not blown by the strong summer meltemi wind, so you should be spared the mixed blessing of being stranded because all sailings have been cancelled for a day or more. Westerly winds, however, may breeze in from Italy, bringing rain (especially out of season), rolling waves and pollution to west-facing beaches. The delight of all these islands is their greenness; the harsh glare of barren rock seen elsewhere is replaced by flowering shrubs and trees.

Don't miss

Corfu
For good reason the best-known and most popular of this group, this lush, green island is blessed with plentiful streams and cypresses. Figs and lemon trees abound, while some of the olive trees are the largest and oldest in Greece. Though heavily developed around its main town, Corfu still has much to offer, especially out of season.
■ Visit Corfu town (Kérkira), with its fine Venetian public buildings and backstreets. The 19th-century British occupation is also evident, with cricket sometimes played on the central green. Pedestrianization has further improved this handsome town, which is ideal for strolling around; don't miss the historic Paleó and Néo Froúrio forts.
■ Stay in Paleokastrítsa, one of the most beautiful resorts, set on a double bay, or the pleasant Kassiópi in the north.
■ Have an overnight stay on the island of Paxos, with its pastel-shaded harbor, Gáois.

Paleokastrítsa, Corfu

THE IONIAN ISLANDS

Lefkáda

A verdant island, reached by crossing a short bridge from the mainland, with some of the most dramatic cliffs and beaches in the country.

■ Enjoy the waves that come rolling in off the Ionian Sea.
■ Visit the main town, Lefkáda, with its attractively painted corrugated iron houses (resistant to earthquakes), near a peaceful lagoon.
■ Visit Vassilikí in the south, a great place for windsurfing.
■ Stay on the east side where the almost land-locked sea makes for perfect sheltered swimming. Take a trip to the pretty islet of Meganíssi.

Kefalonia

This is the largest Ionian island, hard hit by earthquakes, though the northern port of Fiskárdo retains some pretty old-style buildings. The island has some excellent beaches along with the unspoiled and protected landscapes around Mount Enos.

■ Stay in one of the two main towns, Argostóli for a place with nightlife or the quieter Lixoúri.
■ Visit the sandy beaches of Skala, Patís or Makrís Giolós.
■ Visit the cave of Melissani near Sami, which you can see by boat. Incredibly, the water here goes the whole way under the island, reappearing on the other side near Argostóli!
■ Take a day trip to Ithaka, a legendary island which is less visited because of its lack of beaches, but has fine walking country. In Greek legend, Odysseus lived here. Don't miss the cave of the Nymphs near Vathi, where Odysseus is said to have hidden treasure.

Zákynthos (Zante)

This increasingly popular island is best known for its endangered loggerhead turtle, which has produced a mini-boom in eco-tourism. The best thing those concerned about the environment can do is stay off the beaches where the turtles live.

■ Visit Zákynthos town, virtually leveled by an earthquake in the 1950s, but still with hints of its past evident around Plateia Solomou, in the Byzantine Museum and at its huge Venetian fortress.

Corfu town

Central mainland Greece and the Sporades

This area covers the mountainous Stereá Elláda to the north of Athens and the flat agricultural plains of Thessalía, site of two of the country's most stunning locations: the Pélion region and Metéora on the edge of the Píndus mountain range. To the east, the Sporades is a small group of green and sheltered islands.

Don't miss

Delphi
The most magnificent and justly famous Delphi contains the oracle of Apollo, the "navel of the Universe," on the flank of mighty Mount Parnassós. This is where the oracle made her prophecies near the cave where the serpent Python lived.
■ Visit in early morning or evening when the busloads have gone; the view alone is enough to elevate the spirit. Look at the Sanctuary of Athená and the Sacred Precinct above it, including the Temple of Apollo; go on to climb up to the peaceful Stadium.

■ Don't miss the Kastalian Spring, used for purification purposes, and the museum, whose exhibits include the stunning bronze Charioteer.
■ Go down for a swim near Galaxídi, an attractive harbor town on the Gulf of Corinth.

The Karpeníssi area
Often called "the Greek Switzerland," the mountain villages near the town of Karpeníssi are great rural escapes, particularly Mikró Horió (Small Village) and Korisádes, which have fine mansion houses where you can stay (see p48). This wooded area rises to over 6,500 feet and is good for hiking and even rafting (see p90).

the Tholos, Delphi

CENTRAL MAINLAND GREECE AND THE SPORADES

Pélion
This area is quite distinct from anywhere else in the country, with charming villages of handsome, traditional houses dotting the mountainous countryside just a short distance from the beckoning sea and some fine beaches, such as at Plataniá and Maláki.

■ Visit Makrinítsa, clinging to the hillside, and stop under the plane trees in the village square, for a superb view of Volos and out to sea.

■ Go to the traditional villages of Portariá and Zagorá.

■ Take the old train line from Volos to the village of Miliés, a picturesque and memorable ride.

Metéora
A truly spectacular sight near Kalambáka. There are six monasteries dating back to the 14th century – Ayíos Stéfanos is actually a nunnery – precariously located on sheer rock pinnacles. Best visited in autumn or spring, when snow still covers the surrounding mountains, you can see most of them in a day's driving or walking.

Skiáthos
This is the liveliest and most developed of the Sporades islands. The pretty Skiáthos town's nightlife is famous, as is Koukounariés beach, still one of the most beautiful beaches in the Mediterranean. "Banana" beach is a nudists' retreat. Boat trips can take you to quieter beaches on the far side of the tree-clad island.

Skópelos
Skópelos is a slightly quieter but equally verdant island, with two ports, Skópelos town and the port below, Glóssa, both fitting the idyllic Greece of the popular imagination. Walk from Glóssa to the Ayíos Ioánnis monastery, which sits above a quiet beach.

Alónissos
Though less dramatic than others in the group, Alónissos offers a taste of traditional Greece. Visit the restored hillside village of Paliá Alónissos (there was a severe earthquake in 1965), and the beaches of Vithísma and Kokkinókastro.

Skyros
Set apart to the east of the other Sporades, Skyros has its own distinct traditional culture. Skyros town is a fine place, topped by its kástro. See also the memorial to Rupert Brooke, the English war poet. The tranquillity of the island has attracted an "alternative" holistic vacation spot at Atsítsa, which offers various activities such as yoga and writing, and there are some good beaches at Pékfos and Ahíli.

Skiáthos town

Thessaloníki

the White Tower

Europe's 1997 City of Culture (also known in English as Salonica) is a lively city of over a million people. Thessaloníki once had Europe's largest Jewish community, but few remnants of this remain, while a fire in 1917 destroyed much of the historic city. On arrival, its concrete buildings seem as characterless as those in Athens, and indeed it shares some of Athens' congestion and pollution problems. Despite this, its coastal location gives it an airy feel, aided by the extensive green area behind the White Tower and around its excellent Archaeological Museum. Thessaloníki has many examples of Byzantine churches. It is also famous for its many clothes shops and rows of tasteful cafés. Its relatively northern position means that it can be very cold in winter but, like Athens, the warmth of the people make it worth a visit.

Don't miss

The White Tower (Lefkós Pírgos), a handsome post-Byzantine monument on the waterfront that has become Thessaloníki's symbol. Climb to the top for a view over the city.

The Archaeological Museum, especially the Vergína exhibition of gold from the tomb of Philip of Macedon and the ancient Macedonian capital of Aígai (modern Vergina).

The church of Ayía Sophia, dating from the eighth century and modeled on Ayía Sophia in Istanbul.

Ayios Stéfanos Monastery, Meteora

THESSALONIKI

The Rotunda, a Roman monument that was converted into the church of Ayíos Yiórgios and later a mosque. Look for its remaining minaret and its beautiful mosaics.
The Kástra area for a sample of old Thessaloníki, an atmospheric area of old houses and cafes.
A coffee by the Byzantine city ramparts, which circle the old acropolis, in the Eptapírgion area.
The church of Ayíos Dimítrios, originally from the fifth century, but almost entirely rebuilt after the 1917 fire; look for the ancient mosaic of Ayíos Dimítrios, Thessaloníki's protecting saint, which survived the fire.
The Folklore Museum *(Laografikó Mouseío),* an excellent introduction to the crafts, daily work, costumes and women's role in the community.
A visit to Ano Poli, the picturesque old town, with glorious views of the entire city and out to sea.

Have a drink or meal in

Níkis, the waterfront parade that is lined with bars and tavernas.
Olymbos Náoussa, one of the city's most historic restaurants.
Aristotélous Ouzeri on Aristotélous, one of the city's most characterful ouzeries.
For nightlife, try sampling the area around Platéia Navarínou and the area between the White Tower and the Arch of Galerius.

Northern mainland Greece

The diverse and infrequently visited north of Greece includes Epirus (Ipiros), a distinctive region of high villages, graceful old arched bridges and fast-flowing rivers, all dominated by the Píndus Mountains which rise to over 8,200 feet. To the east, Macedonia has been part of modern Greece since 1913, while Thrace (Thraki) has only been part of Greece since 1923. Historically this area was part of Philip of Macedon's territory, and subsequently part of the empire ruled by his son, Alexander the Great. It is an area of a distinct Balkan character, rarely visited by tourists, apart from its main city, Thessaloníki (see above), and Halkidikí.

Don't miss

Ioánnina
The principal town of the region is a historic and attractive one. It is situated on Lake Pamvotída, which has a tranquil offshore island containing five monasteries and its own village. Ioánnina is a good base to see:

■ Métsovo, a winding 35 miles by road up in the mountains. This is the capital of the Vlachs, the nomadic shepherds of the Píndus mountains. Their industries and crafts are most in evidence in the main square and the Métsovo museum.

■ The Zagóri, a beautiful mountainous area of 46 villages (the Zagorohória) north of Ioánnina with fine stone mansions called *arhontiká*. Hiking is a popular way to see the area. Don't miss the dramatic Víkos gorge, though it is probably best to join an organized hike from a travel agency in Ioánnina.

■ Dodóni and the Oracle of Zeus, the second most important oracle in Greece after Delphi. Its elegant theater is the perfect base to see the occasional ancient drama and music performances in summer.

Kastoriá
This is a handsome town of fine Macedonian architecture, *arhontiká* mansions and some 75 churches. It is at the heart of the Greek fur trade; its name comes from the Greek for "beaver." There are no longer beavers in Lake Kastoriá, but take the lakeshore path to see water-snakes and other wildlife.

Grevená
The ecotourism center here organizes trips by jeep and provides

Halkidikí

NORTHERN MAINLAND GREECE

mountain escorts into its beautiful surrounding countryside.

Flórina
The last main town before the border with the Former Yugoslav Republic of Macedonia, a good base to see the wildlife reserves around the lakes of Megáli Préspa and Mikrí Préspa. Visit the attractive village of Psarades and the lovely Edessa, famous for its waterfalls, its ancient stone bridge and riverside parks.

Mount Olympus
The Mountain of the Gods is, at 9,570 feet, Greece's highest peak, best reached from the village of Litóhoro. If you are fit and energetic and have a good map, climb it in the summer months for stunning views and a wealth of wild flowers. Do remember that at such a height the weather can be unpredictable. There are four refuges on the mountain if you need to stay.

Díon
Near Mount Olympus, this site is a vast, partly-excavated ancient city; look for the basilica with fine mosaics, and visit the museum in the modern village of Díon to see the finds from the area.

Pélla
The capital of Macedonia in its prime, and the largest Macedonian city in the time of Philip II and Alexander the Great. Don't miss the famous mosaics, some in the museum opposite, others with finds still on the site.

Halkidikí
■ Kassándra: The first westerly prong of the Halkidikí peninsula is a highly-developed tourist area easily accessible from Thessaloníki, of which Haniótis has one of the best beaches.
■ Sithoniá: This is a greener area with some fine beaches; try those at Paraliá Sikiás or Toróni.
■ Mount Athos: This is a secret and beautiful enclave of monasteries, open to men only, and then only with official permission, though you can stay in villages such as Ouranoupoli, a small resort nearby. Take a boat trip around the spectacular monastic peninsula.

Kavála
One of Greece's most pleasant provincial towns and ports. It has a fine Turkish aqueduct and a Minaret endowed with Islamic inscriptions.
■ See the Egyptian Pasha Mehmet Ali's 18th-century house, in the pleasant old quarter.
■ Visit the Byzantine kástro above it.
■ Visit nearby Philippi, named after Philip of Macedon and where

monastery, Athos peninsula

St. Paul later established the first European Christian church. Look around the theater, the well-preserved public latrines and enjoy the fine view from the Acropolis.

Xánthi
This town in Thráki has a Muslim community complete with minarets, an old quarter and busy market. Go on to the scenic river Néstos valley, either by car or on the train which heads through attractive country villages in the foothills of the Rodópi Mountains.

The Islands of the North Aegean

*T*he islands of this group each have their own unique character and charms. The close proximity of some of them to Turkey has ensured a continuing military presence in the area, but you can also visit Turkey on day trips from the closest islands.

Don't miss

Thássos
Forest fires have destroyed much of the island's pine cover, but it remains one of Greece's most green and beautiful islands. The capital – Liménas or Thássos – clusters around both a new and a charming old harbor.

■ Don't miss the ancient remains including a small theater, with an idyllic view, above Liménas.
■ Visit the east coast's fine beaches and the picturesque hill-villages such as Panagía. A popular spot on the west coast is Limenária with its array of good tavernas and bars.

Límnos
A remote island, although at Mírina, the capital, there are all the facilities of a luxury hotel complex. There is a picturesque small harbor with a castle above the town which offers fine views. Nearby Platí has a good, long beach, while Hortarolímni is a reserve ideal for bird watching.

Lésvos
This large island is dominated by millions of olive trees and oak woods and there is even the remains of a petrified forest. As well as being the birthplace of Sappho and Aesop, it is also that of the naive painter Theóphilos. This 19th-century artist has a museum dedicated to him at Varia near the main Mytlíni town, a good place to sample his original style.

Lésvos

THE ISLANDS OF THE NORTH AEGEAN

■ See the well-conserved village of Mólivos (or Míthimna), a lovely place below a Genoese castle.
■ Visit the superb beach of Vaterá in the south of the island.
■ Stay in Ayiássos for a taste of mountain life in a traditional village of cobbled streets.

Híos (Chios)
This is Greece's richest island and Homer's alleged birthplace. It has prospered from the wealth of its shipping magnates and its unique mastica gum. The island has a wealth of attractive villages and Byzantine monuments.
■ Stay in the capital, Híos, a major port. Among its attractions are the town's bazaar, the *kástro* and the Argénti museum tracing the history of the island's aristocrats.
■ Visit the ancient villages of Armólia, Volissós and Mestá, which grew up on the mastica trade.
■ Swim off the beach of Ayia Markélla, one of the longest and best on the island.
■ Take a day trip or stay on Psará (see p48), a spectacular rocky islet, or even go to Cesme in Turkey, a short ferry ride away.

Sámos
This green island is the most frequented of the group. Its best beaches are in the west. Of its three ports, Pithagório is the island's main resort, while at Váthi, you can see a huge *kóuros* – male nude statue – the largest such effigy to survive from ancient times. Don't forget to try the highly acclaimed Sámos wine.

Holidays, festivals and events

January 1 New Year's Day *(Protochronyá)* sees the *vassilópita* cut, a special loaf containing a coin which brings luck to the finder.

January 6 Epiphany *(Ta Fóta)*, when the priest blesses the waters by casting a cross into the sea at most seaside towns and villages. Brave youths then retrieve it by diving in.

Apókries, Pátras

January 8 The *Gynaecocratía* – in the villages near Xanthi in Thrace, women traditionally take over men's roles for a day, by relaxing in cafés.

February/March Carnival *(Apókries)*, best witnessed in Pátras, the biggest and liveliest event with a parade and fancy dress parties; similar parades can be seen in Moscháto in Athens. In the Monastiráki area of the capital, during the weekend before Clean Monday (see below), you will see people hitting each other with plastic clubs (watch your head, they hurt!). Náoussa in Macedonia, Corfu town and the islands of Kefaloniá and Skyros also have big events, the latter with an ancient "Goat-Dance."

March Clean Monday *(Kathará Deftéra)*, a public holiday that marks the end of carnival time and the start of Lent. Greeks head out into the countryside to fly kites, eat out or have a picnic.

March 25 Independence Day, a holiday commemorating the beginning of the overthrow of the Turks in 1821. There are parades in most places, particularly on Tínos and Idra.

April The Orthodox Easter *(Pásca)* usually falls on a different date from the Catholic Easter, and is Greece's main celebration of the year, with an atmospheric candlelit procession (accompanied by firecrackers) in every town and village at midnight before Easter Sunday. *Mayeirítsa* – a rich soup of lamb intestines – is eaten afterwards and the morning of Easter Day is met with the aroma of spit-roasted lamb being cooked for the great midday feast. Red-dyed hard-boiled eggs are baked into loaves of sweet bread *(tsouréki)*. Red eggs are also knocked together; the uncracked ones bring luck.

April 23 The Feast of St. George; Aráchova has a three-day festival culminating in a race of the village's elderly men in traditional dress.

May 1 May Day *(Protomayá)*, a public holiday traditionally celebrated by picking flowers which are made into wreaths to take back

HOLIDAYS, FESTIVALS AND EVENTS

and hang on doors to welcome the season in.

June The start of the Athens arts festival, with many live performances; look for performances of Classical drama at the theater of Herodes Atticus, or the live jazz at the open-air theater on Likavitos.

July 8 Lifkimi festival in Corfu, with folk dancing.

July 18 The Feast of Prophet Elijah *(Profitís Ilías)*, best seen at the hilltop shrine of Mount Taígetos near Sparti in the Peloponnese.

July Lésvos, at Plomari, which hosts an Ouzo Festival that includes horse races and dancing.

July/August Live theatrical performances at the ancient site of Epidaurus, an extension of the Athens festival.

August Lefkada arts festival, with Greek dance troupes. Balkan Crafts Fair in Volos, with Balkan music and dance.

August 15 Assumption of the Virgin Mary *(tis Panayías)*, best witnessed in Tinos where, at midday, a miraculous icon of the Virgin Mary – found in 1822 – is paraded down to the harbor where people gather for its alleged healing powers.

August 23 Folk festival in Drakiá near Pilion, with traditional costumes on display.

September The Santoríni Music Festival; the Corfu festival – concerts and theatrical performances.

September 8 Battle of the Straits, Spétses, a re-enactment of an 1822 battle followed by fireworks and late-night revelry.

October 28 "No" Day *(í iméra tou Óhi)*, a patriotic holiday celebrating Greek rejection of Mussolini's demands to allow Italian troops "rights of passage" into Greece in 1940, with military parades and folk displays around the country.

November Thessaloníki film festival.

November 17 Polytechnic Day *(í iméra tou Polytechníou)*, which commemorates the Athens Polytechnic students who were killed in 1973 opposing the military junta then in power. In Athens particularly, it is now a day of political demonstration.

December 25 Christmas *(Christoúyenna)*, a less important event than Easter, but still a family occasion with shops and businesses closed.

December 31 New Year's Eve *(Paramoní Protochroniás)* is traditionally a day of carol singing *(ta kálanda)* and, curiously, of playing cards, often for money.

Bare necessities

Greetings

hello or goodbye	γειά σου (singular/informal) **yá sou**
	γειά σας (plural/formal) **yá sas**
good morning	καλημέρα **kaliméra**
good evening	καλησπέρα **kalispéra**
good night	καληνύχτα **kaliníhta**
How are you?	Τι κάνεις (singular/informal)/ κάνετε; (plural/formal) **Ti kánis/kánete?**
Very well, thank you.	Πολύ καλά, ευχαριστώ. **Polí kalá, efharistó.**

Other useful words

please	παρακαλώ **parakaló**
thank you (very much)	ευχαριστώ (πολύ) **efharistó (polí)**
here (you are/it is)	ορίστε **oríste**
You are welcome.	Παρακαλώ. **Parakaló.**
sorry/excuse me	συγνώμη **sighnómi**
It's all right/It doesn't matter	Δεν πειράζει. **Dhen pirázi.**
Don't mention it.	Παρακαλώ. **Parakaló.**
yes/no	ναι/όχι **ne/óhi**
OK	εντάξει **endáxi**
Μάλιστα. **Málista.**	Certainly.
βεβαίως. **Vevéos.**	Yes, of course.

BARE NECESSITIES

phone card

Do you have . . . ?

Do you have any (oranges/postcards)?	Έχετε (πορτοκάλια/κάρτες); Éhete (portokália/kártes)?
Do you have a (map/double room)?	Έχετε (χάρτη/δίκλινο); Éhete (hárti/dhíklino)?

Is there . . . /Are there . . . ?

Is there a (shower/telephone)?	Υπάρχει (ντους/τηλέφωνο); Ipárhi (dous/tiléfono)?
Are there any toilets?	Υπάρχουν τουαλέτες; Ipárhoun toualétes?

Where is/are . . . ?

Where is the (museum/nearest bank)?	Πού είναι (το μουσείο/η πιο κοντινή τράπεζα); Poú íne (to mousío/i pio kondiní trápeza)?
Είναι (ίσια/δεξιά/αριστερά). Ine (ísia/dhexiá/aristerá).	It's (straight ahead/on the right/on the left).

How much?

How much is this?	Πόσο κάνει αυτό; Póso káni aftó?
How much are these?	Πόσο κάνουν αυτά; Póso kánoun aftá?
Nothing else.	Τίποτ άλλο. Tipot állo.

ΓΥΝΑΙΚΩΝ — women's restroom

ΑΝΔΡΩΝ — men's restroom

I'd like

I'd like a ticket to Thessaloniki.	Θέλω ένα εισιτήριο για τη Θεσσαλονίκη. Thélo éna isitírio ya ti Thessaloníki.
I'd like (a kilo/two kilos) of apples.	Μου δίνετε (ένα κιλό/δύο κιλά) μήλα. Mou dhínete (éna kiló/dhío kilá) míla.
I'd like (this one/that one).	Θέλω (αυτό/εκείνο). Thélo (aftó/ekíno).

BARE NECESSITIES

Getting things straight

Pardon?	Ορίστε/Συγνώμη. Oríste/Sighnómi.
Could you say that again, please?	Το επαναλαμβάνετε, παρακαλώ; To epanalamvánete parakaló?
More slowly, please.	Πιο αργά, παρακαλώ. Pió arghá parakaló.
I don't understand.	Δεν καταλαβαίνω. Dhen katalavéno.
I don't know.	Δεν ξέρω. Dhen xéro.

About yourself

My name is . . .	Λέγομαι . . . Léghome . . .
I'm from . . .	Είμαι από . . . Íme apó . . .
Pleased to meet you.	Χαίρω πολύ. Héro polí.
I'm a nurse.	Είμαι νοσοκόμα (f). Ime nosokóma (f).
I'm American.	Είμαι Αμερικάνος (m)/ Αμερικανίδα (f). Ime Amerikános/ Amerikanídha.
I speak a little Greek.	Μιλάω Ελληνικά, λίγο. Miláo Ellinika, lígho.

Changing money

What's the exchange rate for the dollar?	Πόσο έχει το δολλάριο; Póso éhi to dhollário?
I'd like to change $100.	Θέλω να αλλάξω εκατό δολλάρια; Thélo na alláxo ekató dhollária.
Το διαβατήριό σας, παρακαλώ; To dhiavatírió sas, parakaló.	Your passport, please.

Numbers

1	ένας/μία/ένα	énas/mía/éna
2	δύο	dhío
3	τρεις/τρεις/τρία	tris/tris/tría
4	τέσσερις/ τέσσερις/ τέσσερα	tésseris/ tésseris/ téssera
5	πέντε	pénde
6	έξι	éxi
7	εφτά	eftá
8	οχτώ	ohtó
9	εννιά	enniá
10	δέκα	dhéka
11	έντεκα	éndeka
12	δώδεκα	dhódeka
13	δεκατρία	dhekatría
14	δεκατέσσερα	dhekatéssera
15	δεκαπέντε	dhekapénde
16	δεκαέξι	dhekaéxi
20	είκοσι	íkosi
21	είκοσι ένας/μία/ένα	íkosi énas/ mia/éna
30	τριάντα	triánda
40	σαράντα	saránda
50	πενήντα	penínda
60	εξήντα	exínda
70	εβδομήντα	evdhominda
80	ογδόντα	oghdhónda
90	ενενήντα	eneninda
95	ενενήντα πέντε	eneninda pénde
100	εκατό	ekató
200	διακόσια	dhiakósia
208	διακόσια οχτώ	dhiakósia ohtó
300	τριακόσια	triakósia
400	τετρακόσια	tetrakósia
500	πεντακόσια	pendakósia
505	πεντακόσια πέντε	pendakósia pénde
600	εξακόσια	exakósia
700	εφτακόσια	eftakósia
800	οχτακόσια	ohtakósia
900	εννιακόσια	enniakósia
1000	χίλια	hília

The numbers 2, 3, 4, 200, 300, 400, etc, change ending according to what they're referring to. Where three forms are given, this denotes masculine, feminine and neuter forms. See p108 for more details. The currency in Greece is the drachma, **δραχμή**.

Ordinal numbers

1st	πρώτος/ -η/ -ο	prótos
2nd	δεύτερος	dhéfteros
3rd	τρίτος	trítos
4th	τέταρτος	tétartos
5th	πέμπτος	pémptos
6th	έκτος	éktos
7th	έβδομος	évdhomos
8th	όγδοος	óghdhoos
9th	ένατος	énatos
10th	δέκατος	dhékatos

The time

When?	Πότε;	Póté?
What time is it?	Τι ώρα είναι;	Ti óra íne?
It's . . .	Είναι . . .	Ine
midday/midnight	το μεσημέρι/ τα μεσάνυχτα	to mesiméri/ ta mesánihta
(one) o'clock	(μία) η ώρα	(mía) i óra
(two/three) o'clock	δύο/τρεις	dhío/tris
ten past one	μία και δέκα	mía ke dhéka
quarter past two	δύο και τέταρτο	dhío ke tétarto
half past three	τρεις και μισή	tris ke misí
quarter to four	τέσσερις παρά τέταρτο	tésseris pará tétarto
What time does it (leave/arrive)?	Τι ώρα (φεύγει/φτάνει);	Ti óra (févghi/ftáni)?
At two o'clock.	Στις δύο.	Stis dhío.
in the (morning/ evening)	το (πρωί/βράδυ)	to (proí/vrádhi)
yesterday (morning/ evening/afternoon)	χθες το (πρωί/βράδυ/ μεσημέρι)	hthes to (proi/vrádhi/ mesiméri)
last night/ this morning	χθες το βράδυ/Σήμερα το πρωί	hthes to vrádhi/ Simera to proí

BARE NECESSITIES

Days

Monday	Δευτέρα	**Dheftéra**
Tuesday	Τρίτη	**Tríti**
Wednesday	Τετάρτη	**Tetárti**
Thursday	Πέμπτη	**Pémpti**
Friday	Παρασκευή	**Paraskeví**
Saturday	Σάββατο	**Sávato**
Sunday	Κυριακή	**Kiriakí**

Months of the year

January	Ιανουάριος	**Ianouários**
February	Φεβρουάριος	**Fevrouários**
March	Μάρτιος	**Mártios**
April	Απρίλιος	**Aprílios**
May	Μάϊος	**Máios**
June	Ιούνιος	**Ioúnios**
July	Ιούλιος	**Ioúlios**
August	Αύγουστος	**Ávgoustos**
September	Σεπτέμβριος	**Septémvrios**
October	Οκτώβριος	**Októvrios**
November	Νοέμβριος	**Noémvrios**
December	Δεκέμβριος	**Dhekémvrios**

Colors

beige	μπεζ	**bez**	pink	ροζ	**roz**
black	μαύρο	**mávro**	red	κόκκινο	**kókkino**
blue	μπλε	**ble**	white	άσπρο	**áspro**
brown	καφέ	**kafé**	yellow	κίτρινο	**kitrino**
green	πράσινο	**prásino**	dark	σκούρο	**skoúro**
gray	γκρίζο	**grizo**	light	ανοιχτό	**anihtó**

Countries/nationalities

Australia	**Αυστραλία/Αυστραλός** **Afstralía/Afstralós**
Canada	**Καναδάς/Καναδός** **Kanadhás/Kanadhós**
France	**Γαλλία/Γάλλος** **Ghalía/Ghálos**
Germany	**Γερμανία/Γερμανός** **Yermanía/Yermanós**
Great Britain	**Μεγάλη Βρετανία/Βρεττανός** **Megháli Vretanía/Vretanós**
Greece	**Ελλάδα/Ελληνας** **Eládha/'Elinas**
Netherlands	**Ολλανδία/Ολλανδός** **Olandhía/Olandhós**
New Zealand	**Νέα Ζηλανδία/Νεοζηλανδός** **Neazilandhía/Neazilandhós**
(Northern) Ireland	**(Βόρεια)ιρλανδία/ (βόρειο)ιρλανδός (Vória-)irlandhía/ (Vóri-)irlandhós**
Norway	**Νορβηγία/Νορβηγός** **Norviyía/Norvighós**
South Africa	**Νότια Αφρική/ Νοτιοαφρικανός Nótia afrikí/Notioafrikanós**
United States	**Ηνωμένες Πολιτείες/ Αμερικανός Inoménes Políties/ Amerikanós**

BARE NECESSITIES

Language Works

Do you have . . .

1 Buying apples at the market
- **Καλημέρα.**
- ☐ **Καλημέρα. Έχετε μήλα;**
- **Μάλιστα.**
- ☐ **Μου δίνετε δύο κιλά.**
- **Ορίστε.**
- ☐ **Πόσο κάνουν;**
- **Εξακόσιες δραχμές.**
- ☐ **Ευχαριστώ. Γειά σας.**
- **Γειά σας.**

How much do the apples cost?

2 Changing money
- **Γειά σου. Πόσο έχει το δολλάριο;**
- ☐ **Διακόσιες εβδομήντα πέντε δραχμές.**
- **Θέλω να αλλάξω εκατό δολλάρια.**
- ☐ **Εντάξει. Το διαβατήριό σας, παρακαλώ.**

How much is $100 in drachmas?
What does the assistant ask for?

Try it out

Questions and answers

Match the answers to the appropriate questions.
a **Πού είναι το μουσείο;**
b **Πόσο κάνει αυτό;**
c **Έχετε κάρτες;**

1 **Εβδομήντα δραχμές.**
2 **Μάλιστα.**
3 **Αριστερά.**

Summing up

Say these sums – and include the answer!
eg 3 and 4 are . . .
τρία και τέσσερα ίσον εφτά

1 3 and 4 and 9 are . . .
2 10 and 18 are . . .
3 22 and 35 are . . .
4 56 and 65 are . . .
5 49 and 101 are . . .

Time tells

What time is it?
1 08:30
2 05:15
3 20:20
4 14:10

As if you were there

Looking for a bank in Thessaloniki.
- (Say "excuse me." Then say "good morning")
- ☐ **Καλημέρα.**
- (Ask where the bank is)
- ☐ **Ίσια και μετά δεξιά.**
- (Thank him and say goodbye)
- ☐ **Παρακαλώ. Γειά σας.**

Sound Check

x in Greek is like the Scottish "ch" in Loch Ness, eg
έχετε éhete
χρώμα hróma
ευχαριστώ efharistó

Getting around

ΑΝΑΧΩΡΗΣΕΙΣ ΕΣΩΤΕΡΙΚΟΥ ΕΞΟΔΟΙ 1-12

Arriving

Most flights and charter flights fly into Athens or one of the main islands, Corfu, Crete (at Iráklion and Haniá) and Rhodes. Other islands – for instance Sámos, Zákynthos and Santoríni – have direct charters from abroad in season. Thessaloníki carries an increasing amount of international air traffic. It is also possible to arrive in Greece overland by train or road from Bulgaria, the former Yugoslavia and Turkey, though train routes tend to be slow. The most usual entry routes into Greece by sea are via the Italian ports (especially Ancona and Brindisi) into Corfu, Pátras or Igoumenítsa. There are also ferry connections with Turkey (via the islands), Cyprus and Israel.

By sea

Planning boat travel in advance is not always easy, particularly for inter-island or return journeys. A schedule of all routes out of Piraeus (but not back) for the current week is available from the EOT office in Syntagma Square, Athens. The monthly publication *Greek Travel Pages* – available to travel agents – is otherwise the best source of boat times.

Ferry facilities are generally good, especially on main routes. Most ferries have bars and shops, though dining rooms tend to have limited opening hours. Vegetarians in particular are advised to take their own supplies on board on longer journeys. Hydrofoils have few facilities: take your own food and drink.

Ferry ports
Piraeus The main port for the Aegean islands, the nearby Saronic Gulf islands, the Cyclades, the Dodecanese, Crete and the Eastern Aegean.
Rafína To Andros and Tínos and as an alternative departure point to the Cyclades (Rafína is one hour from Athens by car or frequent bus service from Mavromatéon Street).
Pátras To Kefaloniá, Itháki, Corfu and Italy (Pátras is three hours from Athens by coach or Inter-city train).
Killíni To Zákynthos.
Kavála, Macedonia To Thássos and Límnos.
Vólos or Agyíos Constantínos (summer only) To Skiáthos, Skópelos and Alónissos.
Kími, Evía To Skýros.

GETTING AROUND

Some useful inter-island connections

Páros and Náxos are the hub of the ferry system in the Aegean with links to each other and to Ios, Santorini, Crete, Ikaria, Sámos, Síkinos, Folégandros, Astypálea, Kos, Rhodes and (in summer) Amorgós. Páros also links with Síphnos (summer only). The frequency of these links varies from month to month, with July to early September being the peak season.

Hydrofoils ("Flying Dolphins")

These are generally twice as fast – and expensive – as ferries. They are subject to cancellation in very windy weather and not recommended for those prone to travel sickness. The main port is Zéa Marina (a short taxi ride from Piraeus or Paleó Fáliron metro stations).

Cerres Lines serve the main Saronic Gulf islands (except Aegina, served from Piraeus main harbor) and Pórto Héli (near Spétses) and – in summer only – the Eastern Peloponnese, including Náfplion and Monemvasía. There is also a route serving Epidaurus, useful for the summer festival.

The Sporádes islands are served from Ayíos Constantínos, except for Skyros, which is served from Vólos.

Ilios Lines have inter-island connections in the Cyclades: Andros – Ios – Mykonos – Náxos – Páros – Santoríni – Syros and Tínos. They also serve the Dodecanese with inter-island connections to: Rhodes – Kálymnos – Kos – Léros – Níssyros – Pátmos – Symi – Tílos – Sámos.

Europe serve the Ionian Islands, with links between: Pátras – Zákynthos – Itháki and Kefaloniá.

Tickets

■ For ferries, foot passengers do not need to buy tickets in advance, unless a cabin is required. If you want to take a car or motorbike, this will require advance booking and can be expensive. Tickets are available from the numerous ticket agencies in Piraeus, or from travel agents in Athens and around the country. A basic "deck passage" no longer means you have to stay on deck, but is a reasonably cheap way to travel. However, boats on popular routes can get overcrowded; first-class and cabin-class tickets are not much more expensive and worth it to escape this problem.

■ For hydrofoils, tickets can be bought from travel agencies or from specific company booths which can be found near hydrofoil departure points, such as in Zéa near Piraeus and from island ports (see below for company details).

❗ Two tickets to Spetses.
❗ Δύο εισιτήρια για τις Σπέτσες
● **Dhío isitíria ya tis Spétses.**

By air

For a small country, Greece has an exceptional number of airports, with the routes converging on Athens. Prices are quite high and delays are not infrequent. Olympic Airways provides the most comprehensive internal links. All Olympic Airways flights (domestic and international) at Athens airport use the West Terminal (Olympiaki). All other international airlines use the East Terminal but, during the summer, all charter flights are served from the new Charter Terminal, situated adjacent to the East Terminal.

By car

Roads
Despite European Union funds and upgrades, many roads are poor. The National Roads (Ethnikí Odos) is a good-quality system of toll roads, which run from Athens to Pátras and Athens to Lamía and Thessaloníki. An alternative route into the Peloponnese is along the excellent Corinth to Trípoli road.

Safety
The accident toll in Greece is unacceptably high and the driving often fast and aggressive. Crete, in particular, has a reputation for this. Cars tend to pass on either side; a disproportionate number of accidents occur during the afternoon siesta time.
■ Remember that flashing headlights mean "Get out of the way!"
■ In wet weather, Greek roads can be extremely slippery.
■ Beware of inadequately guarded railroad crossings.
■ If traveling at night in the countryside, or at any time in remote areas, don't let your gas tank get too low. The nearest open gas station could be far too far to walk.
■ Gas prices are moderate.

Driving in main cities
Try to avoid leaving Athens and Thessaloníki on a Friday afternoon or evening or returning on a Sunday evening, when traffic is frequently reduced to a snail's pace. Central Athens is probably best avoided altogether. Legal parking spaces are severely restricted and if you are in a rental car, you will be subject to the strict anti-pollution laws which prevent you from driving in the city center before 3 pm on alternate weekdays, the day being determined by your license plate number.

Car rental
The well-known car rental companies have offices in cities and some provincial towns, though car rental is expensive. In addition, numerous local companies operate around the country (a useful list of such companies can be found in the *Greek Travel Pages* at most travel agencies), but be careful to check what you are paying for and make sure you are properly insured.

car rental company

Breakdowns
Most car rental companies have arrangements with road assistance organizations. The main road assistance organization in Greece is ELPA, which has a reciprocal arrangement with similar organizations in other countries. Nonmembers can call up such organizations to deal with breakdowns, though you will be charged accordingly.

GETTING AROUND

By bus (*leoforío*)

On major routes, bus services are punctual, inexpensive and reliable. The buses are operated by KTEL, a syndicate of privately-run companies. The islands and even the remotest villages are covered by their network, although there may be no more than a daily bus to the most outlying places. On main routes, book a seat a few hours in advance at peak holiday times and weekends. One-way tickets are the norm, but you can always purchase a return ticket on arrival at your destination.

■ The major Athens bus station is at Kifissoú 100, for departures to the Peloponnese and Western and Northern Greece.
■ For Central Greece, (Delphi, Aráchova, Kalambáka, Kími and Vólos), go to the bus station at Liossión 260.
■ Thessaloníki's main bus station is on Ikosioktó Oktovríou (28 October Street).

By train

This remains a reasonably cheap and often scenic way to see mainland Greece. The two main routes – Athens to Thessaloníki and Athens to Pátras – offer quick, modern express services, and are faster and more comfortable than bus travel. At terminals, you can book a seat in advance; first-class carriages tend to have more seats available and tickets are not too expensive. If you want to travel a lot by train, you can buy a pass for 10, 20 or 30 days.
■ Sleeper trains are available from Alexandroúpolis to Thessaloníki and Athens and these are modern and comfortable.
■ Other routes are slower, usually on older trains.

funicular railway

Bikes

Most resorts offer mopeds and bikes for rent at reasonable rates, and some can offer motorbikes if you can show a valid license. Bikes are a fun way of getting round, but check that local roads are paved or your routes will be limited. Mopeds are a good way of getting around dirt roads, but be very careful as accidents are all too common and you will have to pay for repairs (to yourself and the moped). Always check the brakes first.

❗ Excuse me, which way is the station?
💬 Που είναι ο σταθμός;
Pou íne o stathmós?

GETTING AROUND

Κέντρο
Center

Phrasemaker

Asking the way

Excuse me.	Συγνώμη. / Sighnómi.
Is there a (pharmacy/park) near here?	Υπάρχει (φαρμακείο/πάρκο) εδώ κοντά; / Ipárhi (farmakío/párko) edhó kondá?
Is the (church/station/port) far?	Είναι (η εκκλησία/ο σταθμός/το λιμάνι) μακριά; / Íne (i eklisía/o stathmós/to limáni) makriá?
Which way is the (tourist office/bank)?	Πού είναι (το τουριστικό γραφείο/η τράπεζα); / Poú íne (to touristikó ghrafío/i trápeza)?
Are there any (restrooms/large shops) near here?	Υπάρχουν (τουαλέτες/μεγάλα καταστήματα) εδώ κοντά; / Ipárhoun (toualétes/meghala katastímata) edhó kondá?
Is this the right way to the (bus station/town center)?	Πάμε καλά για (τον σταθμό λεωφορείων/το κέντρο της πόλης); / Páme kalá ya (ton stathmó leoforíon/to kéndro tis pólis)?
Είναι . . . / Ine	It's . . .
δεξιά/αριστερά / dhexiá/aristerá	on the right/left
μετά (ίσια/ευθεία) / metá (ísia/efthía)	then (straight ahead)
σε εκατό μέτρα / se ekató métra	100 meters away
στη γωνία / sti ghonía	on the corner
Είναι (αρκετά) (κοντά/μακριά). / Ine (arketá) (kondá/makriá).	It is (fairly) (close/far away).
Νάτος! / Nátos!	There it is!
στρίψτε (δεξιά/αριστερά) / strípste (dhexiá/aristerá)	turn (right/left)
περάστε (τη γέφυρα/τον κύριο δρόμο) / peráste (ti ghéfira/ton kirio dhrómo)	cross the (bridge/main road)

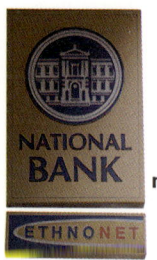

GETTING AROUND

(πρώτο/δεύτερο) (δεξιά/αριστερά) **(próto/dhéftero) (dhexiá/aristerá)**		(first/second) on the (right/left)
μέχρι **méhri**		as far as
στο τέλος του δρόμου **sto télos tou dhrómou**		at the end of the street
κοντά/απέναντι/πίσω από . . . **kondá/apénandi/píso apó . . .**		near/opposite/ behind the . . .

ΜΑΡΙΝΑ ΖΕΑΣ
ZEA MARINA

Places in a town

antiquities	τα αρχαια	**ta arhea**
beach	η παραλία	**i paralía**
bus stop	η στάση	**i stási**
castle	το κάστρο	**to kástro**
cathedral	η μητρόπολη	**i mitrópoli**
church	η εκκλησία	**i ekklisía**
hospital	το νοσοκομείο	**to nosokomío**
market	η αγορά	**i aghorá**
mosque	το τζαμι	**to jamí**
museum	το μουσείο	**to mousío**
park	το πάρκο	**to párko**
parking lot	το πάρκιγκ	**to párking**
Pedestrian zone	Πεζόδρομος	**Pezódhromos**
pharmacy	το φαρμακείο	**to farmakío**
port	το λιμάνι	**to limáni**
restrooms	οι τουαλέτες	**i toualétes**
shopping center	το εμπορικό κέντρο	**to emporikó kéndro**
square	η πλατεία	**i platía**
stadium	το στάδιο	**to stádhio**
(bus/rail) station	ο σταθμός (λεωφορείων/τρένων)	**o stathmós (leoforíon/ thrénon)**
store	το κατάστημα	**to katástima**
street	ο δρόμος/η οδός	**o dhrómos/i odhós**
swimming pool	η πισίνα	**i pisína**
town walls	τα τείχη της πόλης	**ta tíhi tis pólis**

πρός παραλία to the beach

GETTING AROUND

ΕΝΟΙΚΙΑΣΕΙΣ ΑΥΤΟΚΙΝΗΤΩΝ

Renting a car or bike

I'd like to rent a (car/bike/motorbike).	Θέλω να νοικιάσω ένα (αυτοκίνητο/ποδήλατο/μηχανή). **Thélo na nikiáso éna (aftokínito/podhílato/mihaní).**
small/medium/big	μικρό/μέτριο/μεγάλο **mikró/métrio/meghálo**
for (three days/a week)	για (τρεις μέρες/μιά εβδομάδα) **yá (tris méres/miá evdhomádha)**
How much is it per (day/week)?	Πόσο κάνει την (ημέρα/εβδομάδα); **Póso káni tin (iméra/evdhomáda)?**
Is insurance included?	Περιλαμβάνεται η ασφάλεια; **Perilamvánete i asfália?**
Το δίπλωμά σας, παρακαλώ. **To dhiplomá sas parakaló.**	Your driver's license, please.
Για πόσο καιρό; **Yá póso keró?**	For how long?

Road signs

Parking	Στάθμευση	**Státhmefsi**
odd/even	μονά/ζυγά	**moná/zighá**
Keep right	Τηρήστε το δεξιό της οδού	**Tiríste to dhexió tis odhoú**
Use lights	Ανάψτε τα φανάρια σας	**Anápste ta fanária sas**
Right-of-way	Προτεραιότητα	**Protereótita**
No entry	Ο δρόμος είναι κλειστός	**O dhrómos íne klistós**
Entry/Exit	Είσοδος/Έξοδος	**Ísodhos/Éxodhos**
Toll	Διόδια	**dhiódhia**
Detour	Παράκαμψη	**parákampsi**
North	Βορράς	**Vorrás**
South	Νότος	**Nótos**

42

GETTING AROUND

Buying gas

30 liters/5000 drachmas of	τριάντα λίτρα/πέντε χιλιάδες δραχμές	
	triánda lítra/pénde hiliádhes dhrahmés	
unleaded/premium/diesel	αμόλυβδη/σούπερ/πετρέλαιο	
	amólivdhi/super/petréleo	
Fill it up.	Γεμίστε το.	
	Yemíste to.	
Do you have any (air/water/oil)?	Έχετε (αέρα/νερό/λάδι);	
	Éhete (aéra/neró/ladhi)?	

Roadside information

Is this road to . . . ?	Αυτός ο δρόμος βγάζει (στην/στον/στο) . . . ;	
	Aftós o drómos vgázi (stin/ston/sto) . . . ?	
How far is it to . . . ?	Πόσο απέχει . . . ;	
	Póso apéhi . . . ?	
Where is . . . ?	Πού είναι . . . ;	
	Poú íne . . . ?	

Transportation

bike	το ποδήλατο	to podhílato
boat	το καράβι	to karávi
bus	το λεωφορείο	to leoforío
car	το αυτοκίνητο	to aftokínito
ferry	το φέρυ	to féri
hydrofoil	το ιπτάμενο δελφίνι	to iptámeno dhelfíni
plane	το αεροπλάνο	to aeropláno
taxi	το ταξί	to taxí
train	το τρένο	to tréno

Signs

Arrivals	Αφίξεις	
	Afíxis	
Departures	Αναχωρήσεις	
	Anahorísis	
Platform	Αποβάθρα/Πλατφόρμα	
	Apováthra/Platfórma	
Validate your ticket	Ακυρώστε το εισιτήριό σας	
	Akiróste to isitírió sas	
Baggage check	Φύλαξη αποσκευών	
	Fílaxi aposkevón	

ΑΦΙΞΕΙΣ ΕΞΩΤΕΡΙΚΟΥ
ARRIVALS INTERNATIONAL

ΑΠΟΣΚΕΥΑΙ ΥΠΟ ΠΑΡΑΚΑΤΑΘΗΚΗΝ
CONSIGNES — HANDGEPACK

GETTING AROUND

Getting information on buses/trains/boats

Is there a (bus/train/boat) to . . . ?	Υπάρχει (λεωφορείο/ τρένο/καράβι) για . . . ; Ipárhi (leoforío/ tréno/ karávi) ya . . . ?
Does this train go to Patras?	Αυτό το τρένο πάει στην Πάτρα; Aftó to tréno pái stin Pátra?
What time does the bus for . . . (leave/arrive)?	Τι ώρα (φεύγει/φτάνει) το λεωφορείο για . . . ; Ti óra (févyi/ftáni) to leoforío ya . . . ?
What time does the next one leave?	Τι ώρα φεύγει το επόμενο; Ti óra févyi to epómeno?
Which platform?	Από ποιά πλατφόρμα; Apó piá platfórma?
What time does it arrive?	Τι ώρα φτάνει; Ti óra ftáni?
How long does it take?	Πόση ώρα κάνει; Pósi óra káni?
Do you have a schedule?	Έχετε το δρομολόγιο; Éhete to dhromolóyio?
Does this bus go to . . . ?	Αυτό το λεωφορείο πάει στο . . . ; Aftó to leoforío páei sto . . . ?
Can you tell me where to get off?	Πού πρέπει να κατεβώ; Roú prépi na katevó?
Do I have to change?	Πρέπει ν' αλλάξω; Prépi n' alláxo?

κατεβείτε σε . . .	katevíte se . . .	get off at . . .
αλλάξετε σε . . .	alláxete se . . .	change at . . .
Θα σας δείξω.	Tha sas dhíxo.	I'll show you.

44

Buying a ticket

ticket	το εισιτήριο	to isitírio
Where is the ticket office, please?	Πού είναι το εκδοτήριο παρακαλώ;	Poú íne to ekdotírio parakaló?
(single/return) to ...	(απλά/με επιστροφή) για ...	(aplá/me epistrofí) ya ...
for two adults and one child	δύο κανονικά και ένα παιδικό	dhío kaniká ké éna pedhikó
(1st/2nd) class	(πρώτη/δεύτερη) θέση	(próti/dhéfteri) thési
I'd like to reserve a (seat/berth/cabin).	Θέλω να κλείσω μια (θέση/κουκέτα/καμπίνα).	Thélo na klíso mia (thési/koukéta/kabína).

Καπνίζετε;   **Kapnizete?**   Smoking?
Υπάρχει επιβάρυνση.   **Ipárhi epivárinsi.**   There is a charge.

Taking a taxi

Is there a taxi stand near here?	Υπάρχει πιάτσα ταξί εδώ κοντά;	Ipárhi piátsa taxí edhó kondá?
To the airport, please.	Στο αεροδρόμιο, παρακαλώ.	Sto aerodhrómio parakaló.
To this address, please.	Πάω σ'αυτή τη διεύθυνση, παρακαλώ.	Páo s'aftí ti dhiéfthinsi, parakaló.
How (long/far) is it?	(Πόση ώρα/Πόσο απέχει);	(Pósi óra/Póso apéhei)?
How much (is it/will it be)?	Πόσο κάνει;	Póso káni?
Keep the change.	Κρατείστε τα ρέστα.	Kratíste ta résta.
This is for you.	Ορίστε.	Oríste.
Can I have a receipt, please?	Μου δίνετε μία απόδειξη, παρακαλώ;	Mou dhínete mía apódhixi parakaló?

45

GETTING AROUND

Language works

Asking the way

1 Trying to find the station
- □ Συγγνώμη, πού είναι ο σταθμός, παρακαλώ;
- ■ Ίσια, μετά δεξιά, μετά αριστερά και νάτος.
- □ Ευχαριστώ πολύ.
- ■ Παρακαλώ.

The station is on the right/left?

Renting a car

2 Renting a small car
- □ Θέλω να νοικιάσω ένα μικρό αυτοκίνητο.
- ■ Για πόσο καιρό;
- □ Τρεις μέρες.
- ■ Έχουμε Φορντ Φιέστα.

(Έχουμε = we have)

The car you took was a Ford Fiesta: true/false?

Getting gas

3 At a service station
- □ Καλημέρα. Γεμίστε με σούπερ παρακαλώ.
- ■ Μάλιστα. Τίποτ' άλλο;
- □ Να ελέγξετε τα λάδια.
- ■ Εντάξει. Έξι χιλιάδες δραχμές, παρακαλώ.

(να ελέγξετε τα λάδια – check the oil)

Is the oil OK?
The price is . . .

Getting information on boats

4 To Hydra by boat or hydrofoil
- □ Πόσο κάνει το καράβι για την Ύδρα;
- ■ Τρεις χιλιάδες πρώτη θέση.
- □ Πέντε χιλιάδες;
- ■ Και πόσο κάνει το Δελφίνι.
- □ Μία ώρα και το καράβι τρεις;
- ■ Πόση ώρα κάνει το Δελφίνι.

What is the price of tickets by boat/hydrofoil?
How long does the trip take?

Getting information on trains

5 At the station
- □ Τι ώρα φεύγει το τρένο για την Θεσσαλονίκη;
- ■ Στις οχτώ το πρωί.
- □ Και τι ώρα φτάνει;
- ■ Στις δύο.

(πρωί = morning)

The train leaves at . . .
The train arrives at . . .

Buying a ticket

6 Traveling to Spetses by hydrofoil
- □ Τρία εισιτήρια με το Δελφίνι για τις Σπέτσες, παρακαλώ.
- ■ Απλά ή με επιστροφή;
- □ Απλά
- ■ Δεκαοχτώ χιλιάδες δραχμές, παρακαλώ.
- □ Ορίστε.

The price for three tickets is . . .

GETTING AROUND

Try it out

Crossed lines

Match the phrases 1–5 with the appropriate Greek.
1 Turn left
2 800 meters away
3 Small car
4 At 5:15
5 Turn right

a Στις πέντε και τέταρτο.
b Μικρό αυτοκίνητο.
c Στρίψε δεξιά.
d Στρίψε αριστερά.
e Οχτακόσια μέτρα πιο κάτω.

Crossword puzzle

Across
2 a driver's license
4 station
6 Where?
7 far away

Down
1 round-trip ticket
3 bike
5 straight ahead

As if you were there

Inquiring about trains to Pyrghos (**Πύργο**).
- (Ask what time the train leaves for Pyrghos)
- □ Οχτώ και τριάντα το πρωί.
- (Ask how long it takes to Pyrghos)
- □ Οχτώ ώρες.
- (Ask if you need to change)
- □ Ναι, στην Πάτρα.
- (Ask for two round-trip tickets)

Sound Check

υ – this letter is pronounced like a "v" in "**φεύγει**" (févyi) and "**αύριο**" (avrio), but like an "f" in "**ευχαριστώ**" (efharistó).

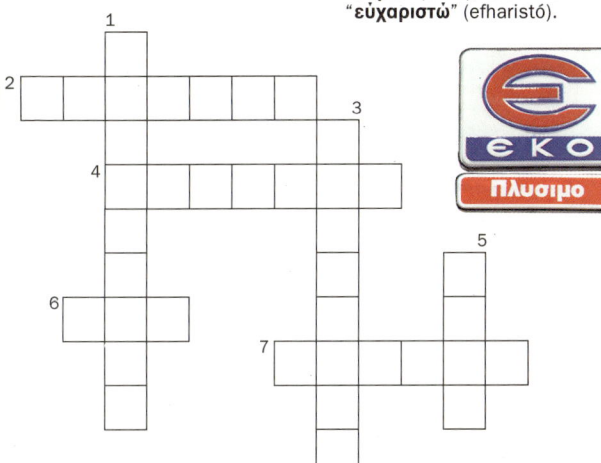

Somewhere to stay

Rentals

Most islands and resorts have a range of rentals available, either houses, apartments, or villas. The latter are usually rented by the week. These usually offer adequate cooking facilities, though remember that on some of the more out-of-the-way islands, the food supplies in the shops may not seem as wide-ranging as what is in the local restaurant. Facilities such as a balcony, a fridge and mosquito-control devices are becoming standard. You will probably find it easiest to book such accommodation through one of the numerous specialist package operators, but make sure you are not put somewhere too remote if you do not have a car. You could also try booking through the local tourist office or even ask in local cafés if places are vacant.

Hotels

In principal resorts and towns, hotels are open all year round. At the top of the range is the "luxury" category, where there is no upper price limit; at the bottom is E class where prices remain modest. Controls exist on prices in the A to E categories and prices should be displayed on the back of room doors. Note that in smaller and remoter resorts, many hotels close for the winter, usually from November to April. Most hotels will offer breakfast and some can offer plans in which meals are included. Some package "resort" hotels may be outside major towns, and, though probably well equipped, may lack character. A good source of hotel information is the *Greek Travel Pages*, a monthly publication available at travel agencies.

> Do you have a double room?
> Έχετε δίκλινο δωμάτιο;
> Éhete díklino dhomátio?

Traditional guesthouses

The EOT renovates historical buildings and rents them out as Traditional Guesthouses or Settlements. These are usually quite upscale establishments or rental options which allow you to stay in comfort in some great locations, such as in tower houses in the Máni (Areópoli and Vathiá) or the beautiful mansions of Pélion's villages, as well as in Korisádes in Central Greece and on Psará near Híos; a full list of these can be supplied by the EOT.

Rooms and boardinghouses

In the summer, there are thousands of rooms (*domátia*) available across the country, officially graded A–C (Α, Β, Γ in Greek). Even in the peak months of July and August you would be unlucky not to find a place to stay if you have not booked in advance. From November to early April, almost all rooms close down. In rooms and *pansións* (guest houses) it is worth bargaining over the room price. This can secure a reduction of up to a third, particularly if you plan to stay more than one night. Prices peak in July and August. In remote locations, a basic cheap room may be inside the family home and have a sink, but the shower and toilet will be separate. Elsewhere expect more modern accommodations with a private bathroom; some even have cooking facilities, but you are rarely offered breakfast.

Youth hostels

These tend to be somewhat unglamorous and some require a Youth Hostel Card. They can be found in Athens, Thessaloníki, Pátras, Náfplion, Mikínes (Mycenae), Olympia, Delphi and at Mount Olympus, plus on the islands of Crete, Santoríni and Corfu. Note that some of these have a night curfew. Additionally, Athens has a number of Student Hostels – not only for students – that provide cheap, basic accommodations.

Camping

Hundreds of campsites exist around the country, varying considerably in size and range of facilities. Camping is generally very safe – thefts rarely occur – and open to camper vans. Some campsites are open all year round. Only a few cater for the disabled. EOT offices can provide a campsite guide. With a little Greek, the annual *Odigós Camping* (Camping Greece) is very useful. It is widely available in the country from newsstands. Camping in the wild is technically illegal, although it is not uncommon.

How much is it per night?
Πόσο κοστίζει τη βραδιά;
Póso kostízi ti vradhiá?

Children

Most hotels cater to children, though few offer babysitters. Cribs can usually be supplied, but it is best to order these in advance where possible. Take great care with elevators, many of which do not have inner doors.

Phrasemaker

Finding a place

Is there a (hotel/campsite) near here?	Υπάρχει (ξενοδοχείο/κάμπιγκ) εδώ κοντά; Ipárhi (xenodohohío/camping) edhó kondá?
Do you have a (single/double/triple) room?	Έχετε (μονόκλινο/δίκλινο/τρίκλινο) δωμάτιο; Éhete (monóklino/dhíklino/tríklino) dhomátio?
for two nights	για δύο βραδιές ya dhío vradhiés
for four people	για τέσσερα άτομα ya téssera átoma
two adults and two children	δύο μεγάλους και δύο παιδιά dhío meghálous ke dhío pedhiá
May I see the room?	Μπορώ να δω το δωμάτιο; Boró na dho to dhomátio?
How much is it per night?	Πόσο κοστίζει τη βραδιά; Póso kostízi ti vradhiá?
Do you have anything cheaper?	Έχετε κάτι φθηνότερο; Éhete káti fthinótero?
I'll take it.	Θα το πάρω. Tha to páro.
We'll think about it.	Θα δούμε. Tha dhoúme.

Πόσες βραδιές; Póses vradhiés?	How many nights?
Πόσα άτομα; Pósa átoma?	How many people?
Συγνώμη, είμαστε γεμάτοι. Sighnómi, ímaste yemáti.	I'm sorry, we're full.
τα παιδιά μισοτιμής ta pedhiá misotimís	children half-price

Places to stay

Campsite	**Κάμπιγκ**	**Kamping**
Hotel	**Ξενοδοχείο**	**Xenodhohío**
Boardinghouse	**Πανσιόν**	**Pansión**
Rooms	**Δωμάτια**	**Dhomátia**
Beds	**Κρεβάτια**	**Krevátia**
Youth Hostel	**Ξενώνας νεότητας**	**Xenónas neótitas**

Rentals	**Διαμερίσματα με πολυκουζίνα**
	Dhiamerísmata me políkouzína
Apartments for rent	**Ενοικιάζονται διαμερίσματα**
	Enikiázonde dhiamerísmata

Specifications

with a (bathroom/shower)	**με (μπάνιο/ντους)**
	me (bánio/dous)
with a (single/double/child's) bed	**με (μονό/διπλό/παιδικό) κρεβάτι**
	me (monó/dhipló/pedhikó) kreváti
Is breakfast included?	**Περιλαμβάνεται το πρωινό;**
	Perilamvánete to proinó?
το πρωινό/ο φόρος	breakfast/tax
to proinó/o fóros	
(δεν) περιλαμβάνεται	is (not) included
(dhen) perilamvánete	

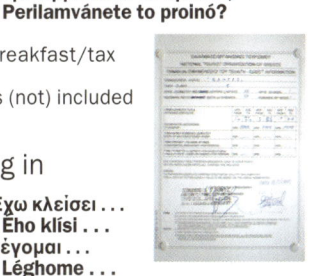

Checking in

I have a reservation . . .	**Έχω κλείσει . . .**
	Ého klísi . . .
My name's . . .	**Λέγομαι . . .**
	Léghome . . .
Where can I park?	**Πού μπορώ να παρκάρω;**
	Poú boró na parkáro?
Το όνομά σας, παρακαλώ	Your name, please.
To ónomá sas, parakaló	
το διαβατήριό σας	your passport
to dhiavatírió sas	
Παρακαλώ συμπληρώστε το έντυπο.	Please fill in the form.
Parakaló sibliróste to éndipo.	
Αριθμός δωματίου . . .	Room number . . .
Arithmós dhomatíou . . .	
Ποιός είναι ο αριθμός του αυτοκινήτου σας;	What is your license plate number?
Piós íne o arithmós tou aftokinítou sas?	

Services

What time is breakfast?	Τι ώρα είναι το πρωινό; **Tí óra íne to proinó?**
Is there (an elevator/air conditioning)?	Υπάρχει (ασανσέρ/αιρ κοντίσιον); **Ypárhi (asansér/air condition)?**
Do you have an iron?	Έχετε σίδερο; **Éhete sídhero?**
Where is the (restaurant/bar)?	Πού είναι το (εστιατόριο/μπαρ); **Roú íne to (estiatório/bar)?**
How do I get an outside number?	Πώς παίρνω εξωτερική γραμμή; **Pós pérno exoterikí ghramí?**

εφτά και τριάντα με δέκα και τριάντα **eftá ke triánda me dhéka ke triánda**	from 7:30 to 10:30
Είναι στον τρίτο όροφο. **Íne ston tríto órofo.**	It's on the third floor.
Πάρτε το μηδέν. **Párte to midhén.**	Dial zero.

SOMEWHERE TO STAY

Problems

The (telephone/shower) isn't working.	Το (τηλέφωνο/ντους) δεν δουλεύει. **To (tiléfono/dous) dhen dhoulévi.**
There is a problem with . . .	Υπάρχει πρόβλημα με . . . **Ypárhi próvlima me . . .**
How do you work the (shower/blinds)?	Πώς λειτουργεί το (ντους/ρολό); **Pós litouryí to (dous/roló)?**
There is no (soap/water).	Δεν έχει (σαπούνι/νερό). **Dhen éhi (sapoúni/neró).**
There are no (towels/pillows/blankets).	Δεν έχει (πετσέτες/μαξιλάρια/κουβέρτες). **Dhen éhi (petsétes/maxilária/kouvértes).**
Θα στείλουμε κάποιον. **Tha stíloume kápion.**	We'll send somebody.
Θα σας φέρω. **Tha sas féro.**	I'll get you some.

In your room

blanket	η κουβέρτα	**i kouvérta**
blinds	τα ρολά	**ta rolá**
door	η πόρτα	**i pórta**
cold/hot water	το κρύο/ζεστό νερό	**to krío/zestó neró**
faucet	η βρύση	**i vrísi**
heating	η θέρμανση	**i thérmansi**
key	το κλειδί	**to klidhí**
lamp	η λάμπα	**i lámba**
light	το φως	**to fos**
lock	η κλειδαριά	**i klidhariá**
phone	το τηλέφωνο	**to tiléfono**
pillow	το μαξιλάρι	**to maxilári**
sheet	το σεντόνι	**to sendóni**
shower	το ντους	**to dous**
shutters	τα πατζούρια	**ta patzoúria**
standard lamp	το λαμπατέρ	**to lambatér**
toilet paper	το χαρτί τουαλέτας	**to hartí toualétas**
towel	η πετσέτα	**i petséta**
TV	η τηλεόραση	**i tileórasi**
wash basin	ο νιπτήρας	**o niptíras**
window	το παράθυρο	**to paráthiro**

SOMEWHERE TO STAY

Asking for help

Could I have a wake-up call at . . . ?	**Μπορείτε να με ξυπνήσετε στις . . . ;** **Boríte na me xipnísete stis . . . ?**
Do you have a safety deposit box?	**Έχετε θυρίδα;** **Éhete thirídha?**
Do you have a map of the town?	**Έχετε χάρτη της πόλης;** **Éhete hárti tis pólis?**
Could you recommend a restaurant?	**Μπορείτε να μου συστήσετε ένα εστιατόριο;** **Boríte na mou sistísete éna estiatório?**
Could you order me a taxi?	**Μπορείτε να καλέσετε ένα ταξί;** **Boríte na kalésete éna taxí?**
Is there somewhere to park?	**Μπορώ να παρκάρω κάπου;** **Boró na parkáro kápou?**

Checking out

I'd like to pay the bill.	**Θέλω να πληρώσω τον λογαριασμό.** **Thélo na pliróso ton loghariasmó.**
by traveler's check/ by credit card/cash	**με ταξιδιωτική επιταγή/με πιστωτική κάρτα/μετρητά** **me taxidhiotikí epitayí/me pistotikí kárta/metritá**
I think there is a mistake.	**Νομίζω ότι υπάρχει κάποιο λάθος.** **Nomízo óti ipárhi kápio láthos.**

Ποιόν αριθμό δωματίου; **Pión arithmó dhomatíou?**	Which room number?
Πώς θα πληρώσετε; **Pós tha pilrósete?**	How are you going to pay?
Υπογράψτε εδώ. **Ipoghrápste edhó.**	Sign here.

SOMEWHERE TO STAY

Camping Naoussa

Campsites

Have you got space for a (car/camper/tent)?	Έχετε χώρο για (ένα αυτοκίνητο/ένα τροχόσπιτο/μία σκηνή); **Éhete hóro ya (éna aftokínito/éna trohóspito/mía skiní)?**
How much does it cost?	Πόσο κοστίζει; **Póso kostízi?**
Where are the (showers/trash cans/restrooms)?	Πού είναι (τα ντους/οι σκουπιδοντενεκέδες/οι τουαλέτες); **Poú íne (ta dous/i skoupidhontenekédhes/i toualétes)?**
Is there a (laundry/shop/swimming pool)?	Υπάρχει (πλυντήριο/μαγαζί/πισίνα); **Ipárhi (plyndírio/maghazí/pisína)?**

Facilities

air conditioning	το αιρ κοντίσιον	**to air condítion**
balcony	το μπαλκόνι	**to balkóni**
bar	το μπαρ	**to bar**
fitness center	το γυμναστήριο	**to yimnastírio**
garden	ο κήπος	**o kípos**
hotel plan with one meal included	η πανσιόν ημιδιατροσή	**i pansión imidhiatrosí**
pool	η πισίνα	**i pisína**
restaurant	το εστιατόριο	**to estiatório**
room service	το ρουμ σέρβις	**to roum sérvis**
sauna	η σάουνα	**i sáouna**
tennis court	το γήπεδο τένις	**to yípedho ténis**
terrace	η βεράντα	**i veránda**

Rentals

I've rented a villa.	Νοίκιασα μία βίλα. **Níkiasa mía víla.**
How does the (heating/water) work?	Πώς λειτουργεί το (καλοριφέρ/νερό); **Pós litouryí to (kalorifér/neró)?**

55

Language works

Finding a place to stay

1 Renting a double room on an island
- ☐ **Καλημέρα σας, έχετε δίκλινο δωμάτιο;**
- ■ **Μάλιστα. Πόσες βραδιές;**
- ☐ **Τρεις. Πόσο κοστίζει τη βραδιά;**
- ■ **Οχτώ χιλιάδες.**
- ☐ **Έχετε κάτι φθηνότερο;**
- ■ **Μάλιστα. Έξι χιλιάδες χωρίς μπάνιο.**
- ☐ **Εντάξει. Θα το πάρω.**

(**χωρίς** = without)

How much is the cheaper room?
Does it have a bathroom?

Checking in

2 You have a reservation
- ☐ **Έχω κλείσει ένα μονόκλινο.**
- ■ **Το όνομά σας, παρακαλώ.**
- ☐ **Ελένη Οικονόμου.**
- ■ **Το διαβατήριό σας, παρακαλώ.**
- ☐ **Ορίστε.**
- ■ **Ο αριθμός δωματίου είναι διακόσια τριάντα.**

You are asked to give your name and passport: true/ false?
Your room number is 250: true/false?

Services

3 Making inquiries about breakfast in your hotel
- ☐ **Καλημέρα. Πού είναι το εστιατόριο;**
- ■ **Στον τρίτο όροφο.**
- ☐ **Τι ώρα είναι το πρωινό;**
- ■ **Εφτά και τριάντα με δέκα και τριάντα.**

The restaurant is on the second floor: true/false?
Breakfast is served from 7:30 to 9:30: true/false?

Asking for help

4 Requesting a wake-up call
- ☐ **Μπορείτε να με ξυπνήσετε αύριο το πρωί;**
- ■ **Μάλιστα. Τι ώρα θέλετε;**
- ☐ **Στις έξι.**
- ■ **Βεβαίως.**

What time will the receptionist wake you up?

At the campsite

5 Trying to find a space at a campsite
- ☐ **Γειά σας. Έχετε χώρο για ένα τροχόσπιτο;**
- ■ **Συγγνώμη, είμαστε γεμάτοι.**
- ☐ **Υπάρχει άλλο κάμπινγκ εδώ κοντά;**
- ■ **Μάλιστα. Στα Λουτρά.**

Where is there an alternative campsite?

SOMEWHERE TO STAY

Try it out

Match them up

Match the Greek word with the correct type of accommodation.
1 διαμερίσματα
2 πανσιόν
3 κρεβάτια
4 κάμπιγκ
5 δωμάτια
6 ξενοδοχείο

a campsite
b hotel
c boardinghouse
d rooms
e beds
f apartments

Jumbled conversation

Correct the word order of each sentence to make a dialogue at a hotel reception desk.
■ Σας καλημέρα.
□ Κλείσει έχω μονόκλινο ένα.
■ Ονομά σας παρακαλώ το.
□ Σμιθ Τζον.
■ Το παρακαλώ σας διαβατήριο.
□ Ορίστε!
■ Το αυτό συμπληρώστε έντυπο!

As if you were there

Asking for rooms at a boardinghouse
□ **Καλημέρα.**
■ (Say hello and ask if there are any double rooms available)
□ **Μάλιστα. Με μπάνιο;**
■ (Say yes and ask how much it costs per night)
□ **Οχτώ χιλιάδες τη βραδιά. Πόσες βραδιές;**
■ (Say two nights)

Sound Check

The Greek letter "ψ" is pronounced "ps," as in lapse. Common words including this letter are **ψάρι** (psári/fish) and **ψωμί** (psomí/bread).

Buying things
Shops

Shopping hours are still very much dictated by the afternoon siesta and are slightly complicated by the fact that different types of shops have different hours, with some variation from summer to winter:

■ Stores open every morning (Monday–Saturday), close in the afternoons but reopen on Tuesday, Thursday and Friday from about 5:30 pm to 8:00 or 8:30 pm.
■ Exceptions to this are supermarkets, department stores and shops catering to tourists, which stay open continuously and often on Sundays in the resorts.

florist

One of the most useful Greek shops is the stand (*to períptero*) which works on the tardis principle: they contain far more than their size seems to allow. They are a newsstand, a tobacco shop, and a general store, usually with public phones, and they sell stamps and telephone cards too.

🎙 How much is it?
🗣 Πόσο κάνει;
● *Póso káni?*

Buying souvenirs

Athens claims to contain the largest area of souvenir, crafts and jewelry shops in the world in the area spanning the Plaka and Monastiráki, including the Monastiráki Flea Market. The latter includes what is known as the *Yousouroúm*, a Sunday junk market where you can find Greek tapes and records, clothing, pottery and just about anything else. Prices are definitely negotiable. Unofficially, you can also bargain in many of the regular shops in the area; a few words of Greek will definitely be to your advantage!

The Sunday flea market in Pireus and the bazaar area of Thessaloníki are also good for souvenirs. Elsewhere, most tourist destinations have a range of souvenir shops, some good quality, others decidedly tacky.

Best-value goods

Jewelry, silver and gold Greece is a relatively cheap place to buy precious metals and jewelry, away from the most commercial tourist spots. Rhodes and Kos enjoy lower taxes than elsewhere and can be cheaper for jewelry, crystals, etc. Voukourestíou Street in Athens is also a good place to head, as is Venizélou/Ermoú in Thessaloníki and Ioánnina in Epirus, and the main centers on Páros, Crete and Corfu.

Clothes Basic clothes and leather goods are relatively inexpensive throughout Greece. For designer labels, head for Kolonáki and the plush suburb of Kifissiá in Athens, but be prepared for high prices here. Leather goods and shoes are reasonable in Crete; Haniá is the center for buying *stivánia*, the traditional Cretan leather boots.

🎙 I'm just looking, thank you.
🗣 Απλά κοιτάω, ευχαριστώ.
● *Aplá kitáo, efharistó.*

58

BUYING THINGS

Honey and olives Greek honey has a justifiably good reputation; Santoríni, Tílos, Halki, Attiki and Athos all produce good local honey. The best olives come from Kalamáta (Peloponnese) and Anfissa (near Delphi). Greek olive oil is less internationally famous but is of high quality.

Handwoven rugs and fabrics Many areas sell locally made and attractive rugs and handwoven fabrics, such as Santoríni, Náxos, Corfu and Skópelos. Métsovo, in Epirus, is one of the best places, where traditional weaving methods are still used; *flokátes* rugs and handwoven shoulder bags are a speciality of Aráchova, also in Epirus. Colourful *pataniés* fabrics can be found in Crete.

Embroidery This remains a cottage industry in many areas. Good-quality embroidery can be bought on Náxos, Santoríni, Corfu, Lefkáda and Skyros.

Pottery and ceramics As well as the cheap tourist trinkets, you can find attractive, good-value local ceramics especially in Páros, Skyros, Crete, Aegina, Lésvos and Híos.

Wood carvings Areas that retain traditional wood-carving techniques include Crete, Arcadía in the Peloponnese, Lésvos, Ioánnina in Epirus, Corfu (olive wood carvings) and Skyros (wooden stools).

Metalwork Good buys include copper goods in Skyros, brass bells in Epirus, bronze handicrafts in Thessalía and knives from Crete.

Buying food

■ Permanent markets can be found in all main provincial towns and are recommended for good, fresh produce. In Athens, the atmospheric central meat, fish, fruit and vegetable markets are all on Athinás Street north of Monastiráki; in Thessaloníki, head for the Modiano. The main markets of Iráklion and Haniá in Crete are also colorful. Additionally, most areas have a weekly fruit and vegetable street market.

■ Produce shops (*to manáviko*) are usually reliable, though the traditional Greek grocery store (*to bakáliko*) is now less common than the ubiquitous supermarkets.

■ Supermarkets should cover most of your food needs. However, if you are traveling with a baby, bring all food supplies with you – baby food ranges are limited and relatively expensive. There are also plenty of mini-markets, especially in resorts, and these are usually crammed with goods, including many familiar imported foodstuffs.

1ος ΟΡΟΦΟΣ FLOOR

Phrasemaker

Phrases to use anywhere

Do you have any (cheese/jeans)?	Μήπως έχετε (τυρί/τζιν); Mípos éhete (tirí/dzin)?
A . . . , please.	Ένα . . . , παρακαλώ. Éna . . . , parakaló.
How much (is it/are they)?	Πόσο (κάνει/κάνουν); Póso (káni/kánoun)?
This one/That one.	Αυτό/Εκείνο. Aftó/Ekíno.
That's all, thanks.	Αυτά, ευχαριστώ. Aftá, efharistó.
How much is that (altogether)?	Πόσο κάνει αυτό (όλα μαζί); Póso káni aftó (óla mazí)?
Can I pay (with traveler's checks/by credit card)?	Μπορώ να πληρώσω με (ταξιδιωτικές επιταγές/πιστωτική κάρτα); Boró na pliróso me (taxidhiotikés epitayés/pistotiki kárta)?

2ος ΟΡΟΦΟΣ FLOOR

Να σας βοηθήσω; Na sas voithíso?	Can I help you?
Δυστυχώς όχι. Dhistihós óhi.	I'm afraid not.
Ορίστε. Oríste.	Here you are.
Τίποτ' άλλο; Típot állo?	Anything else?
Όλα . . . μαζί. Óla . . . mazí.	That's . . . altogether.
Φτάνει; ftáni?	Enough?

Names of shops

bakery	ο φούρνος	o foúrnos
bookstore	το βιβλιοπωλείο	to vivliopolío
butcher	το χασάπικο	to hasápiko
cake shop	το ζαχαροπλαστείο	to zaharoplastío
clothing store	το κατάστημα νεωτερισμών	to katástima neoterismón
dairy shop	το γαλακτοπωλείο	to galaktopolío
department store	το πολυκατάστημα	to polikatástima

ΝΙΚΗΤΑΣ PATISSERIE

ΦΟΥΡΝΟΣ

BUYING THINGS

fish shop	το ιχθυοπωλείο	to ihthiopolío
grocery store	το παντοπωλείο	to pandopolío
hairdresser	το κομμωτήριο	to kommotírio
newsstand	το περίπτερο	to períptero
pharmacy	το φαρμακείο	to farmakío
produce shop	το μανάβικο	to manáviko
supermarket	το σούπερμαρκετ	to soupermárket
travel agency	το ταξιδιωτικό πρακτορείο	to taxidhiotikó praktorio

Food shopping

How much (is it/are they) a kilo?	Πόσο (κάνει/κάνουν) το κιλό;	Póso (káni/kánoun) to kiló?
One kilo of (apples/tomatoes), please.	Ένα κιλό (μήλα/ντομάτες), παρακαλώ.	Éna kiló (míla/domátes), parakaló.
half a kilo of (cherries/flour)	μισό κιλό (κεράσια/αλεύρι)	misó kiló (kerásia/alévri)
100 grams of candy	εκατό γραμμάρια καραμέλες	ekató ghrammária karaméles
a slice of . . .	μια φέτα . . .	mia féta . . .
three slices of . . .	τρείς φέτες . . .	tris fétes . . .
Can I try (some/a piece)?	Μπορώ να δοκιμάσω (λίγο/ένα κομμάτι);	Boró na dhokimáso (ligho/éna kommáti)?
A bit more.	Λίγο ακόμα.	Lígho akóma.
A bit less.	Πιο λίγο.	Pio lígho.

Πόσο θέλετε;	Póso thélete?	How much would you like?
Έχουμε μόνο . . .	Éhoume móno . . .	We've only got . . .

kilo	κιλό	kiló
half-kilo	μισό κιλό	misó kiló
100 grams	εκατό γραμμάρια	ekató ghrammaria
bottle	μπουκάλι	boukáli
jar	βάζο	vázo
packet	πακέτο	pakéto
can	κονσέρβα	konsérva
sachet	σακκουλάκι	sakkouláki
quarter-kilo	τέταρτο	tétarto

Buying clothes

I'm just looking, thank you.	Απλά κοιτάω, ευχαριστώ. **Aplá kitáo, efharistó.**
I'd like a (shirt/pair of pants).	Θέλω ένα (πουκάμισο/παντελόνι). **Thélo éna (poukámiso/pantelóni).**
My size is . . . 40.	Το νούμερό μου είναι . . . σαράντα. **To noúmero mou íne . . . saránda.**
May I try (it/them) on?	Μπορώ να (το/τα) δοκιμάσω; **Boró na (to/ta) dhokimáso?**
It's a little (big/small).	Είναι λίγο (μεγάλο/μικρό). **Íne lígho (meghálo/mikró).**
They're a little (big/small).	Είναι λίγο (μεγάλα/μικρά). **Íne lígho (meghála/mikrá).**
Do you have anything (smaller/cheaper)?	Έχετε κάτι (μικρότερο/φθηνότερο); **Éhete káti (mikrótero/fthinótero)?**
Do you have the same in (yellow/green)?	Έχετε το ίδιο σε (κίτρινο/πράσινο); **Éhete to ídhio se (kitrino/prásino)?**
I like (it/them).	Μου (αρέσει/αρέσουν). **Mou (arési/arésoun).**
I don't like (it/them).	Δεν μου (αρέσει/αρέσουν). **Dhen mou (arési/arésoun).**
I'll take (it/them).	Θα (το/τα) πάρω. **Tha (to/ta) páro.**
I'll think about it.	Θα το σκεφτώ. **Tha to skeftó.**
Τί (νούμερο/χρώμα); **Ti (noúmero/hróma)?**	What (size/color)?
Πώς σας (φαίνεται/φαίνονται); **Pos sas (fénete/fénonte)?**	How do you like (it/them)?

Clothes and accessories

bag	η τσάντα	i tsánda
bathing suit/trunks	το μαγιώ	to mayió
belt	η ζώνη	i zóni
cardigan	η ζακέτα	i jakéta
clothes	τα ρούχα	ta roúha
dress	το φουστάνι	to foustáni
handkerchief	το μαντήλι	to mantíli
hat	το καπέλο	to kapélo
jacket	το σακκάκι	to sakáki
overcoat	το παλτό	to paltó
pants	το παντελόνι	to pantelóni
sandals	τα πέδιλα	ta pédhila
scarf	το κασκόλ	to kaskól
shirt/blouse	το πουκάμισο	to poukámiso
shoes	τα παπούτσια	ta papoútsia
shorts	το σόρτς	to sórts
skirt	η φούστα	i foústa
socks/stockings	οι κάλτσες	i káltses
sunglasses	τα γυαλιά ηλίου	ta yialiá ilíou
sweater	το πουλόβερ	to pullóver
T-shirt	το T-σερτ	to T-sert
underwear	τα εσώρουχα	ta esórouha

(for colors see p32)

BUYING THINGS

Department store

Where is the . . . department?	Πού είναι το τμήμα . . . ; Poú íne to tmíma . . . ?
Where can I find the shoes?	Πού είναι τα παπούτσια; Poú ine ta papoútsia?
Is there an elevator?	Υπάρχει ασανσέρ; Ipárhi asansér?
στο (ισόγειο/πρώτο όροφο/ δεύτερο όροφο) sto (isóyio/próto órofo/ dhéftero órofo)	on the (first/ second/third) floor
στο υπόγειο sto ipóyio	in the basement

Buying stamps

How much is a stamp for (the USA/England)?	Πόσο κάνει ένα γραμματόσημο για την (Αγγλία/Αμερική); Póso káni éna ghrammatósimo ya tin (Amerikí/Anglía)?
for a (letter/postcard)	για (γράμμα/κάρτα) ya (ghrámma /kárta)
Two (. . .drachma) stamps, please.	Δύο γραμματόσημα (. . . δραχμών) παρακαλώ. Dhío ghrammatósima (. . . drahmón) parakaló.
I'd like to send this to (Australia/Austria).	Θέλω να στείλω αυτό στην (Αυστραλία/Αυστρία). Thélo na stílo aftó stin (Afstralía/Afstría).

Photography

A roll of 33 mm film for (prints/slides).	Ένα φιλμ 33 χιλιοστυν για (φωτογραφίες/διαφάνειες). Ena film 33 hilioston yia (fotoghrafíes/diafánies).
batteries	μπαταρίες bataríes
Can you develop this?	μπορείτε να το εμφανίσετε; boríte na to emfanísete?
When will it be ready?	Πότε θα είναι έτοιμο; Póte tha íne étimo?
Σήμερα/Αύριο. Símera/Ávrio.	Today/Tomorrow.
Σε (μια ώρα/τρεις ώρες). Se (mia óra/tris óres).	In (1 hour/3 hours).

BUYING THINGS

Groceries

beer	η μπύρα	i bíra
cheese	το τυρί	to tirí
chocolate	η σοκολάτα	i sokoláta
coffee	ο καφές	o kafés
crackers	τα μπισκότα	ta biskóta
dish-washing liquid	το υγρό για τα πιάτα	to ighró yia ta piáta
eggs	τα αυγά	ta avgá
fruit	τα φρούτα	ta froúta
ham	το ζαμπόν	to zambón
honey	το μέλι	to méli
jam	η μαρμελάδα	i marmeládha
laundry detergent	το απορρυπαντικό	to aporipantikó
lemonade	η λεμονάδα	i lemonádha
milk	το γάλα	to gála
orange juice	ο χυμός πορτοκάλι	o hymós portokáli
orange soda	η πορτοκαλάδα	i portokaládha
pepper	το πιπέρι	to pipéri
salt	το αλάτι	to aláti
sugar	η ζάχαρη	i záhari
tea	το τσάι	to tsái
vegetables	τα λαχανικά	ta lahaniká
water	το νερό	to neró
wine	το κρασί	to krasí
yogurt	το γιαούρτι	to yiaoúrti

Household

deodorant	το αποσμητικό	to aposmitikó
diapers	η πάνα	i pána
sanitary napkins	η σερβιέτα	i serviéta
shampoo	το σαμπουάν	to sampouán
soap	το σαπούνι	to sapoúni
tissues	τα χαρτομάντηλα	ta hartomándila
toothbrush	η οδοντόβουρτσα	i odhondóvourtsa
toothpaste	η οδοντόπαστα	i odhondópasta

BUYING THINGS

Specialties

bread	το ψωμί	to psomí
cakes in syrup	τα γλυκά του ταψιού	ta ghlyká tou tapsioú
cookies	τα κουλουράκια	ta koulourákia
pastries	οι πάστες	i pástes
sweet bread	το τσουρέκι	to tsouréki
toast	οι φρυγανιές	i frighaniés
taramosolata	η ταραμοσαλάτα	i taramosaláta

Fruit

apple	το μήλο	to mílo
apricot	το βερύκοκο	to veríkoko
banana	η μπανάνα	i banána
cherry	το κεράσι	to kerási
fig	το σύκο	to síko
grape	το σταφύλι	to stafíli
lemon	το λεμόνι	to lemóni
melon	το πεπόνι	to pepóni
orange	το πορτοκάλι	to portokáli
peach	το ροδάκινο	to rodhákino
pear	το αχλάδι	to ahládhi
strawberry	η φράουλα	i fráoula
tangerine	το μανταρίνι	to mandaríni
tomato	η ντομάτα	i domáta
watermelon	το καρπούζι	to karpoúzi

Vegetables

cabbage	το λάχανο	to láhano
carrots	τα καρότα	ta karóta
cucumber	το αγγούρι	to agoúri
eggplant	η μελιτζάνα	i melitzána
garlic	το σκόρδο	to skórdho
green beans	τα φασολάκια	ta fasolákia
lettuce	το μαρούλι	to maroúli
mushrooms	τα μανιτάρια	ta manitária
okra	οι μπάμιες	i bámies
onions	τα κρεμμύδια	ta kremídhia
oregano	η ρίγανη	i ríghani
peas	τα μπιζέλια	ta bizélia
peppers	οι πιπεριές	i piperiés
potatoes	οι πατάτες	i patátes
spinach	το σπανάκι	to spanáki
zucchini	το κολοκύθι	to kolokíthi

(See also Menu reader p84)

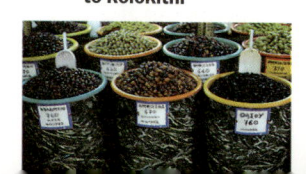

BUYING THINGS

Newsstand (períptero)

book	το βιβλίο	to vivlío
candy	οι καραμέλες	i karaméles
chewing gum	η τσίχλα	i tsíhla
cigarettes	τα τσιγάρα	ta tsighára
American newspapers	οι Αμερικανικές εφημερίδες	i Amerikanikés efimerídhes
magazine	το περιοδικό	to periodhikó
matches	τα σπίρτα	ta spírta
pen	το στυλό	to styló
postcard	η κάρτα	i kárta
stamp	το γραμματόσημο	to ghramatósimo
telephone card	η τηλεκάρτα	i tilekárta

Souvenirs

alabaster objects	το αλάβαστρο	to alávastro
backgammon	το τάβλι	to távli
brass	ο μπρούτζος	o broútzos
ceramics	το κεραμικά	to keramiká
cologne	η κολόνια	i kolónia
embroidery	τα κέντημα	ta kéndima
fur	η γούνα	i ghoúna
icon	η εικόνα	i ikóna
jewelry	τα κοσμήματα	ta kosmímata
plate	το πιάτο	to piáto
rug	το χαλί	to halí
silverware	τα ασημικά	ta asimiká
vase	το βάζο	to vázo
worry beads	το κομπολόι	to komboloí

BUYING THINGS

Language works

Shopping

1 Buying fruit at the local market
- Να σας βοηθήσω;
- Ένα καρπούζι, δύο κιλά ντομάτες και τρία λεμόνια, παρακαλώ.
- Ορίστε.
- Πόσο κάνουν αυτά όλα μαζί;
- Χίλιες διακόσιες δραχμές.
- Ευχαριστώ. Γειά σας.
- Γειά σας, ευχαριστώ.

The total price is......

Food shopping

2 Buying food for a picnic
- Μήπως έχετε ζαμπόν;
- Ναι. Πόσο θέλετε;
- Ένα τέταρτο ζαμπόν και εκατό γραμμάρια τυρί.
- Τίποτ' άλλο;
- Ναι, λίγη ταραμοσαλάτα.
- Φτάνει;
- Ναι, ευχαριστώ. Αυτά.

Does the shop have everything you want?

Buying clothes

3 Buying a pair of pants
- Θέλω ένα μαύρο παντελόνι.
- Τι νούμερο;
- Σαράντα τέσσερα.
- Έχουμε μόνο μπλε και καφέ.
- Μπορώ να δοκιμάσω το καφέ;

Do they have black pants?

BUYING THINGS

Try it out

Jumbled conversation

Put the words in each sentence in the correct order to make a dialogue at a stand.

- Εφημερίδα μια παρακαλώ Αγγλική.
- Τίποτα ορίστε άλλο;
- Ένα πακέτο πόσο τσιγάρα κάνει.
- Πεντακόσιες παρακαλώ δραχμές.

Something missing

Fill in the missing vowels to make words for food.

ν_ρ_ = νερό

1 τ_ρ_
2 γ_ _ _ _ρτ_
3 ζ_μπ_ν
4 ψ_μ_
5 π_π_ν_
6 ντ_μ_τ_

As if you were there

Food shopping
You are in a small grocery store
- (Ask for 250 grams of cheese, two hundred grams of ham, and some taramosalata)
- **Φτάνει η ταραμοσαλάτα;**
- (Ask for a little bit more)
- **Τίποτ' άλλο;**
- (Ask for three lemons, and a bar of chocolate. And say "that's all")
- **Τρεις χιλιάδες δραχμές, παρακαλώ.**
- (Say "there you are")
- **Ευχαριστώ, τα ρέστα σας.**
- (Say goodbye)

Sound Check

"μπ" at the beginning of a word in Greek is pronounced as the English "b" in bed. Examples of this are **μπέζ** (beige) and **μπισκότα** (biscuit)

Café life

Cafés do not get going particularly early, as breakfast is not considered a meal, more a time to have coffee and perhaps cake or *kouloúri* (a hooped biscuit). However, after around 8 am, hotels and most cafés in resorts can offer tourist breakfasts of bread and jam, eggs, yogurt, toast and coffee. Cafés and bars also get busy after siesta time at 6 pm and after dinner until the small hours. Most cafés and restaurants are fairly smoke-filled, as Greece does not have no-smoking areas and a large majority of Greeks are heavy smokers.

Cafés and snacks

■ **Cafés** are now widespread and are what Greek life is all about - sipping a drink and watching the world go by. They also serve food and are open all day and late into the night.

■ **A kafeneió** opens relatively early and is the traditional old-fashioned Greek coffee shop, catering for the older generation of local Greek men, though women are increasingly frequenting them too. Larger ones can offer tea and drinks (alcoholic and soft). Few serve food, but they are the perfect place for a drink stop and get particularly lively after the afternoon siesta (indeed many cafés close from around 2 to 6 pm).

■ **A zaharoplastío** (patisserie or pastry shop) is your best bet for a non-tourist breakfast, cake or dessert. Most are carry-out only, for coffee, yogurt or pastries often made on the premises. Greeks go to these for dessert after their evening meal.

■ **A galaktopolío** is a dairy shop selling yogurt, custard and ice cream to eat there or carry out.

■ **A foúrnos** (bakery) sells - along with bread - milk, yogurt, drinks, ice cream, some types of sweets and biscuits and delicious cheese pies (*tirópites*), which make the perfect snack.

I'll have a Greek coffee.
Ελληνικό καφέ, παρακαλώ.
Ellinikó kafé, parakaló.

Bars and more snacks

■ **An ouzeri** provides *mezédhes* (snacks and tidbits) with ouzo, or beer if you prefer. Try asking for a *pikilía* which is a selection of octopus, sausage, cheese, salad, etc.

■ **A biraría** is a beer bar serving draft beer and snacks such as grilled sandwiches. Some upscale areas have beer gardens and these offer a variety of imported beers.

Where are the restrooms?
Που είναι οι τουαλέτες;
Pou íne i toualétes?

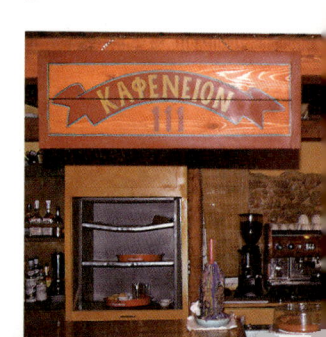

CAFÉ LIFE

Phrasemaker

Asking what there is

Do you have any (sandwiches/grapefruit juice)?	Έχετε (σάντουιτς/χυμό γκρέιπ φρουτ); **Éhete (sandwich/himó grape fruit)?**
What (snacks/cakes) do you have?	Τι (πρόχειρο φαγητό/γλυκά) έχετε; **Ti (próhiro fayitó/ghliká) éhete?**
What soft drinks do you have?	Τι αναψυκτικά έχετε; **Ti anapsiktiká éhete?**
Ορίστε. Παρακαλώ! **Oríste. Parakaló?**	What would you like?
Συγγνώμη, μας τελείωσε. **Sighnómi, mas telíose.**	I'm sorry, we've run out.

Ordering

I'll have a (cheese sandwich/pancake), please.	(Ένα σάντουιτς με τυρί/Μια κρέπα), παρακαλώ. **(Éna sandwich me tirí/Mia krépa) parakaló.**
I'll have (coffee with cream/an orange juice).	(Καφέ με γάλα/χυμό πορτοκάλι). **(Kafé me ghála/hymó portokáli).**
I'll have (strawberry/lemon) ice cream, please.	Παγωτό (φράουλα/λεμόνι), παρακαλώ. **Paghotó (fráoula/lemóni), parakaló.**
This one/That one.	Αυτό/Εκείνο. **Aftó/Ekíno.**
Με (πάγο/λεμόνι); **Me (págho/lemóni)?**	With (ice/lemon)?
Ανθρακούχο η εμφιαλωμένο; **Anthrakoúho i emfialoméno?**	Carbonated or noncarbonated?
Ποιό; **Pió?**	Which one?
Πληρώστε στο ταμείο, παρακαλώ. **Plilróste sto tamío parakaló.**	Please pay at the register.
Είναι σελφ-σέρβις. **Íne self service.**	It's self-service.
Τι παγωτό θέλετε; **Ti paghotó thélete?**	Which flavor of ice cream?
Τίποτ' αλλο; **Típot' allo?**	Anything else?

71

CAFÉ LIFE

Other useful phrases

Where are the restrooms, please?	Πού είναι οι τουαλέτες, παρακαλώ;	Poú íne i toualétes parakaló?
Is there a telephone?	Υπάρχει τηλέφωνο;	Ipárhi tiléfono?
How much is it?	Πόσο κάνει;	Póso káni?
Here you are.	Ορίστε.	Oríste.

Soft drinks

coke	η κόκα κόλα	i kóka kóla
fruit juices	οι χυμοί φρούτων	i himí froúton
ice-cream soda	η άις κριμ σόδα	i íce cream sódha
iced coffee	ο φραπέ	o frapé
iced tea	το παγωμένο τσάι	to paghoméno tsái
lemonade	η λεμονάδα	i lemonádha
milkshake	το μίλκσέικ	to milkshake
mineral water	το μεταλλικό νερό	to metallikó neró
orange juice	ο χυμό πορτοκάλι	o hymó portokáli
orange soda	η πορτοκαλάδα	i portokaládha
lemon/peach/ strawberry	λεμόνι/ροδάκινο/ φράουλα	lemóni/rodhákino/ fráoula
sherbet	η γρανίτα	i ghraníta
soda water	η σόδα	i sódha
tonic water	το τόνικ	to tónic

CAFÉ LIFE

Alcoholic drinks

aperitif	το απεριτίφ	to aperitíf
beer/lager	η μπύρα	i bíra
brandy	το κονιάκ	to cognac
draft/bottle	χύμα/μπουκάλι	híma/boukáli
gin	το τζιν	to gin
ouzo	το ούζο	to oúzo
whisky	το ουίσκυ	to whiskey
wine	το κρασί	to krasí
red/rosé/white	κόκκινο/ροζέ/άσπρο	kókino/rosé/áspro

Hot drinks

capuccino	ο καπουτσίνο	o capuccíno
hot chocolate	η σοκολάτα	i sokoláta
coffee	ο καφές	o kafés
coffee (hot)	ο νες (ζεστό)	o nes (zestó)
decaffeinated	ο ντεκαφεινέ	o dekafiné
espresso	ο εσπρέσο	o esprésso
Greek coffee	ο ελληνικός καφές	o ellinikós kafés
tea	το τσάι	to tsái

Snacks

cheese pie/	η τυρόπιτα/	i tirópita/
spinach pie	η σπανακόπιτα	i spanakópita
gyros	ο γύρος	o yíros
sandwich (hot/cold)	το σάντουιτς (ζεστό/κρύο)	to sandwich (zestó/krío)
with (ham/cheese/ sausage)	με (ζαμπόν/τυρί/ λουκάνικο)	me (zambón/tirí/ loukániko)
omelette	η ομελέτα	i omeléta
pancake	η κρέπα	i krépa
spaghetti	η μακαρονάδα	i makaronádha
toast	η φρυγανιά	i friganiá
waffle	η βάφλα	i váfla

CAFÉ LIFE

Cakes

almond	η αμυγδάλου	i amigdhálou
baklava	ο μπακλαβάς	o baklavás
cake	η τούρτα	i toúrta
cakes in syrup	τα γλυκά του ταψιου	ta ghliká tou tapsioú
chocolate	η σοκολατίνα	i sokolatína
chocolate-covered nougat	η νουγκατίνα	i nougatína
cookie	το κουλουράκι	to kouloúraki
cracker	το μπισκότο	to biskóto
cream	η κρέμα	i kréma
cream pie	η μπουγάτσα	i bougátsa
cream-puff	το προφιτερόλ	to profiteról
whipped cream	η σαντιγί	i sandiyí
milk pie	το γαλακτομπούρεκο	to galaktoboúreko
sponge cake	το ραβανί	to ravaní
walnut pastry roll	το καταίφι	to kataífi

Ice cream

apricot	το βερύκοκο	to veríkoko
banana	η μπανάνα	i banána
cherry	το κεράσι	to kerási
chocolate	η σοκολάτα	i sokoláta
cone	το χωνάκι	to honáki
cup	το κυπελλάκι	to kipeláki
peach	το ροδάκινο	to rodhákino
pistachio	το φυστίκι	to fistíki
strawberry	η φράουλα	i fráoula
vanilla	η κρέμα	i kréma
wafer	το μπισκότο	to biskóto

Language works

Asking what there is

1 Asking about ice cream
- □ Τί παγωτά έχετε;
- ■ Σοκολάτα, φράουλα, κρέμα.
- □ Έχετε φυστίκι;
- ■ Μας τελείωσε.
- □ Μία σοκολάτα, παρακαλώ.
- ■ Μάλιστα.

Do they have any pistachio?

Ordering a snack

2 In a sandwich bar
- □ Ένα σάντουιτς με τυρί και ζαμπόν, παρακαλώ.
- ■ Μάλιστα. Τίποτ' άλλο;
- □ Ένα καταΐφι.
- ■ Μάλιστα. Πληρώστε στο ταμείο, παρακαλώ.

You pay the waiter: true/false?

Ordering drinks

3 Buying drinks for four
- □ Ορίστε. Παρακαλώ.
- ■ Τί μπύρα έχετε;
- □ Αμστελ, Κορόνα και Χάινεκεν.
- ■ Δύο μπουκάλια Αμστελ, παρακαλώ.
- □ Τίποτ' άλλο;
- ■ Ένα ούζο με πάγο, και ένα ελληνικό καφέ.
- □ Δύο χιλιάδες δραχμές, παρακαλώ.
- ■ Ορίστε. Ευχαριστώ.

How much do the drinks cost?

Try it out

Know your drinks

Put the following drinks into the correct category: a) cold drinks, b) hot drinks, c) alcoholic drinks
φραπέ, ούζο, κρασί κόκκινο, ροφήματα, γρανίτα, καφές, τσάι, χυμός πορτοκάλι, τζιν, καπουτσίνο, μπύρα

Jumbled conversation

Put the words in each sentence in the correct order to make a dialogue in a bar.
- □ Μπύρα έχετε χαίρετε τι;
- ■ Και Κορόνα Αμστελ.
- □ Μπουκάλια παρακαλώ τρία Αμστελ.
- ■ Αλλο ορίστε τίποτα;
- □ Πάγο ούζο με.

As if you were there

In a café
- □ (Ask what kind of cakes they have)
- ■ Σοκολατίνα, Νουγκατίνα, Αμυγδάλου.
- □ (Ask if they have any sherbet)
- ■ Μας τελείωσε.
- □ (You order chocolate cake and an orange soda)
- ■ Μάλιστα.

Sound check

It is important to notice the use of accents in Greek words. They tell you which syllable to stress. For example:
παρακαλώ parakaló the stress falls on "ló" at the end of the word
μπύρα bíra the stress falls on the first syllable "bí"
σοκολάτα sokoláta the stress falls on the third syllable "lá."

Practice on these words:
λεμονάδα, τυρί, σόδα, κρασί, εσπρέσο

75

Eating out

For the Greeks, eating out is a great and inexpensive social event. Lunch is available from around 12 to as late as 5 pm. Restaurants will serve dinner from around 7 pm but only tourists will eat before 9 pm. Greeks spend time over this main meal which often goes on beyond midnight.

Where to eat

■ **An estiatório** (restaurant) is commonly found in towns; in tourist places, *estiatória* serve up food pretty much from noon onwards, though not usually dessert. You may be invited into the kitchen to choose your dish. Unlike many countries, there is not usually a great difference between restaurants in terms of being up- or downscale. Almost all will serve up good-quality food in an informal atmosphere. Even the nicest place will welcome children and large groups. To be sure of a good restaurant, go to the one with the most locals.

■ **A taverna** can offer *tis óras*, meaning meat grilled or fried on the spot (unlike an *estiatorió* where food is often on display already cooked). A taverna does not always open at lunchtime, except on the islands. Many have a garden or outdoor space to sit in and, if you are lucky, large barrels of wine inside. At some tavernas, a number of appetizers and side dishes may be brought for you to select from a large tray, before the main course comes. Fruit may be served for dessert. Tavernas stay open late; 1 or 2 am is quite usual.

■ **A psistariá** (grill house) can be identified by the smell of sizzling meat. They are especially popular in inland market and mountain towns and serve meat dishes and simple salads. Again, do not expect dessert.

■ **A psarotavérna** is a taverna specializing in fish dishes and they open for lunch. Common, as you would expect, at ports.

Types of food

Greek food has a mixed reputation; many visitors complain that it is dull, but this is probably because many resorts fall back on low-quality international fast foods and remoter places can only offer what is available locally. Nevertheless, with its fresh fish and seafood, high-quality meats and middle-eastern influenced vegetable and bean dishes, Greek food can be decidedly varied. Fish such as swordfish, mullet, sea-bream, lobster and prawns are common, if not as cheap as you may expect. Meat tends to be lamb, pork or veal. Soups, casseroles and stews are popular, while game and offal is prevalent on the mainland. Most dishes are cooked liberally with olive oil; you may wish to ask for salads without it if you feel things are too oily. Also, do not be surprised if your food is lukewarm, as many dishes are cooked in the morning and allowed to cool; hot food is considered bad for the digestion.

Dishes not to be missed

μπακλαβάς

Souvláki, tender meat (usually pork) served on a skewer, either as a main dish or with pita or ordinary bread as a snack. Chicken souvláki, served with bacon and green peppers, is also good.
Mousakás, made with eggplant, ground beef, and bechamel sauce. A variant of *mousakás* is *papoutsákia* (literally "small shoes").
Dolmádes, rice flavored with dill or mint and wrapped in grape leaves, sometimes with ground beef. It may be served with *avgolémono* sauce (egg and lemon).
Stifádo, a traditional beef casserole, with baby onions in a rich sauce.
Briám, a good vegetarian stew that includes zucchini, eggplant, tomatoes, and sometimes peppers.
Yemistá, peppers and tomatoes stuffed with delicately flavored rice.
Bakaliáros skordaliá, cod cooked in batter and served with an often wickedly strong garlic sauce. Ensure at least two of you order this to avoid becoming a social outcast afterwards!

Horiátiki saláta, Greek "village" salad – tomatoes, cucumber, onions, green peppers and feta cheese. The oil and oregano bring out the flavor beautifully.
Baklavá, a well-known dessert consisting of thin layers of pastry and nuts soaked in honey syrup, though you will find it in *zaharoplastía* (sweet shops or patisseries) rather than restaurants.
Loukoumádes, honey fritters with cinnamon.

What do you recommend?
Τι συστήνετε;
Ti sistínete?

Drinks not to be missed

Ouzo This aniseed-flavored national specialty is sometimes diluted with water, and should be accompanied by a small plate of mezé such as octopus or cheese. It is made from the pulp remaining at the end of the wine-making process.
Tsípouro or Rakí A fierce version of ouzo.
Retsína A pine-resinated wine which people identify as "the flavor of Greece": it can be an acquired taste.
Barreled wine (*híma* or *varelíssio*) This can be resinated or non-resinated, white or red and can be the cheapest and one of the best drinks around. It is served by the kilo – a large jug – or half-kilo.
Bottled wines Greek wines are little known outside the country but there is a large variety and something to suit all palates. Look for *Tsántali* (including *Agiorítiko* and *Makedonikós*), *Hatzimicháli*, *Domaine Carras* and the inexpensive *Logádo*. Two good taverna standards are Lac de Roches and Cambás. If you want to sample a local wine, ask for *dópio krasí*.

Metaxá The national brandy is a perfect nightcap, available as a three, five or seven-star drink. The three is on the rough side, the seven is smooth.

Greek coffee (*Ellinikó*): This is dark and thick, made in a tiny pot and served in a small cup. Order it without sugar (*skéto*), medium sweet (*métrio*) or sweet (*glykó*). Sip it when the grounds have settled.

Iced coffee (*Frappé*): The best way to drink coffee in the Greek summer, this strong, iced coffee can be served with evaporated milk and sugar. For a luxury version try asking for *frappé mé pagotó* (with a scoop of vanilla ice-cream) or for a deluxe *frappé mé Baileys* (with Baileys).

> The bill, please.
> Τον λογαριασμό, παρακαλώ.
> Ton loghariasmó, parakaló.

Regional specialties

Attiki and around Athens *thalassiná tou Egéou*, (seafood risotto); *achiní yemistí* (stuffed sea urchins); *fistíkia tís Aeginas* (pistachio nuts from Aegina); *retsína Attikis* (retsina).

The Cyclades *góuna* (sun-dried and grilled mackerel); *kolokitholoúlouda tiganitá* (fried zucchini flowers); *kítro* (a sweet citrus liqueur from Naxos); *kopanistí* (a strong cheese salad); *amygdalotá* (almond candy); *loukoúmia* (Turkish Delight from Syros).

Dodecanese *zimarikó me yiaourti* (pasta with yogurt and onion); *koriandolíno* (a fruit liqueur from Rhodes); *marída pikántiki* (spicy whitebait).

Crete *Mavro Romeika* (a strong red wine); *salingária stifádo* (snail stew); boiled goat; *stáka* (fried cheese); *kalitsoúnia* (sweet cheese pies with cinnamon and mint).

The Peloponnese *Mavrodáphne* (a sweet red wine); *Achaia Clauss* (wine from Patras); *gourounopoúla* (spit-roast pork traditionally cooked when there is local celebration or festival); *pastélli* (sesame sweets).

Ionian islands *Robóla* (red wine from Kefalonía); *graviéra* (a Gruyere-type cheese); *bourdhéto* (rock fish with tomato and onion sauce); *mandoláto* (nougat from Zakinthos).

Northern and central mainland Greece *fasoláda* (bean soup); *spetzofái* (spicy pork sausages with green peppers); *péstrofa* (trout); *kokorétsi* (spit-roast liver); *kakaviá* (fish soup); *bougátsa* (cream pies); *mídhia* (mussels in batter); *kourabiédes* (an almond shortbread); *tyrópsomo* (cheese bread); *halvá*.

Sporádes *garídes saganáki* (prawns baked with cheese and tomatoes); lobsters and seafood; prunes and almonds from Skopelos.

North-east Aegean *láhano me kimá* (cabbage with ground beef), *mastíka* (a sweet aperitif from Hios); *filiani dolmádes* (minced meat rolled in onion skins), anchovies and ouzo from Lésvos.

> More water, please.
> Ακόμα λίγο νερό, παρακαλώ.
> Akóma ligho neró, parakaló.

vineyards, Halkidiki

χταπόδι drying

Phrasemaker

Finding somewhere to eat

Is there a good restaurant near here?	Υπάρχει ένα καλό εστιατόριο εδώ κοντά; Ipárhi éna kaló estiatório edhó kondá?

Arriving

A table for (2/4), please.	Ένα τραπέζι για (δύο/τέσσερις), παρακαλώ. Éna trapézi ya (dhío/téseris), parakaló.
We have a reservation for . . .	Έχουμε κλείσει για . . . Éhoume klísi ya . . .

At the restaurant

bowl	το μπολ	to bol
bread	το ψωμί	to psomí
cheese	το τυρί	to tyrí
cup	το φλιτζάνι	to flidzáni
fork	το πιρούνι	to pirúni
glass	το ποτήρι	to potíri
knife	το μαχαίρι	to mahéri
napkin	η πετσέτα	i petséta
oil	το λάδι	to ládhi
pepper	το πιπέρι	to pipéri
plate/dish	το πιάτο	to piáto
salt	το αλάτι	to aláti
saucer	το πιατάκι	to piatáki
spoon	το κουτάλι	to koutáli
teaspoon	το κουταλάκι	to koutaláki
vinegar	το ξύδι	to xídhi
water	το νερό	to neró

Asking about the menu

The menu, please.	Τον κατάλογο, παρακαλώ. Ton katálogho, parakaló.
Is there a "menu of the day"/ set menu?	Υπάρχει 'μενού'/ταμπλ ντοτ; Ipárhi menoú/table-d'hote?
What is . . . ?	Τί είναι . . . ; Tí íne . . . ?
What do you recommend?	Τί συστήνετε; Tí sistínete?

79

EATING OUT

τζατζίκι

What's the local specialty?	Ποιά είναι η ντόπια σπεσιαλιτέ; **Piá íne i dópia spesialité?**
Do you have . . . ?	Έχετε . . . ; **Éhete . . . ?**
Is the tip included?	Περιλαμβάνεται το φιλοδώρημα; **Perilamvánete to filodhórima?**

Ordering

(I'll have) . . . , please.	(Μου φέρνετε) . . . , παρακαλώ. **(Mou férnete) . . . , parakaló.**
. . . as a(n) (appetizer/main course/dessert)	. . . για (πρώτο πιάτο/κύριο πιάτο/επιδόρπιο) **. . . ya (próto piáto/kírio piáto/epidhórpio)**
No dessert, thank you.	Όχι επιδόρπιο, ευχαριστώ. **Ohi epidhórpio, efharistó.**

Τί θα πάρετε; **Ti tha párete?**	What would you like?
Είστε έτοιμοι να παραγγείλετε; **Íste étimi na paragílete?**	Are you ready to order?
Σήμερα έχουμε . . . **Símera éhoume . . .**	Today we have . . .
Πώς θέλετε να το ψήσουμε; **Pos thélete na to psisoume?**	How would you like it done?
Θέλετε επιδόρπιο; **Thélete epidhórpio?**	Would you like a dessert?
Τί θα πιείτε; **Ti tha píite?**	To drink?
Συγγνώμη, δεν έχουμε . . . **Sighnómi, dhen éhoume . . .**	Sorry, we don't have any . . .
Το φιλοδώρημα (δεν) περιλαμβάνεται. **To filodhórima (dhen) perilamvánete.**	The tip is (not) included.
Καλή όρεξη. **Kalí órexi.**	Enjoy your meal.

(see p109 for information on the different forms of the singular and plural)

(see Café life p72–73 for how to order drinks)

Eating preferences

I'm allergic to . . .	Είμαι αλλεργικός σε . . . Íme alerghikós se . . .
I'm vegetarian.	Είμαι χορτοφάγος. Íme hortofághos.
Does it contain . . . ?	Περιέχει . . . ; Periéhi . . . ?

During the meal

Excuse me!/Waiter!	Συγγνώμη!/Παρακαλώ! Sighnómi!/Parakaló!
I didn't order . . .	Δεν παρήγγειλα . . . Dhen paríngila . . .
Another (bottle of) . . .	Ακόμα (ένα μπουκάλι) . . . Akóma (éna boukáli) . . .
More bread, please.	Ψωμί, παρακαλώ. Psomí, parakaló.
It's (delicious/very good).	Είναι (νοστιμότατο/πολύ ωραίο). Íne (nostimótato/polí oréo).
It's (cold/underdone).	Είναι (κρύο/άψητο). Íne (krío/ápsito).
Where are the restrooms?	Πού είναι οι τουαλέτες; Poú íne i toualétes?

Ποιανού είναι το κοτόπουλο; Pianoú íne to kotopoulo?	Who is the chicken for?
Όλα εντάξει; Óla endáxi?	Everything OK?
Πώς είναι το . . . ; Pos íne to . . . ?	How's the . . . ?
Τίποτ' άλλο; Típot' állo?	Anything else?

Paying

The bill, please.	Τον λογαριασμό, παρακαλώ. Ton loghariasmó, parakaló.
Do you take credit cards?	Παίρνετε πιστωτικές κάρτες; Pérnete pistotikés kártes?
Is the tip included?	Περιλαμβάνεται το φιλοδώρημα; Perilamvánete to filodhórima?
There's a mistake, I think.	Υπάρχει κάποιο λάθος, νομίζω. Ipárhi kápio láthos, nomízo.
We didn't have (any beer/a dessert).	Δεν πήραμε (μπύρα/επιδόρπιο). Dhen pírame (bíra/epidhórpio).
A receipt, please.	Μία απόδειξη, παρακαλώ. Mía apódhixi, parakaló.

EATING OUT

Language works

Asking about the menu

1 Asking what they have
- ■ Παρακαλώ.
- □ Έχετε μουσακά;
- ■ Συγνώμη, δεν έχουμε. Έχουμε παπουτσάκια.
- □ Τί είναι αυτό;
- ■ Μελιτζάνες γεμιστές με κιμά.
- □ Ωραία. Παπουτσάκια, παρακαλώ.

(Ωραία = fine)

What is papoutsakia?

Ordering a meal and drinks

2 In a restaurant
- □ Ορίστε.
- ■ Μία ταραμοσαλάτα, τζατζίκι σαλάτα και δύο μπριζόλες, παρακαλώ.
- □ Τί σαλάτα θέλετε;
- ■ Χωριάτικη.
- □ Τί θα πιείτε;
- ■ Μισό κιλό ρετσίνα, και ένα μπουκάλι μεταλλικό νερό.

Do they have everything you want?

Eating habits

3 Asking about vegetarian options
- □ Είμαι χορτοφάγος. Έχετε λαδερά;
- ■ Σήμερα έχουμε φασολάκια, μπάμιες, μελιτζάνες.
- □ Φασολάκια και μία μπύρα.

How many vegetarian options do they have?

Paying

4 Asking for the bill
- ■ Όλα εντάξει;
- □ Είναι νοστιμότατο.
- ■ Τίποτ' άλλο;
- □ Όχι ευχαριστώ. Τον λογαριασμό, παρακαλώ.

What does the waiter ask you?

5 There's a problem with the bill
- □ Υπάρχει κάποιο λάθος. Δεν πήρα κοκκινιστό.
- ■ Συγνώμη. Ορίστε.
- □ Ευχαριστώ, και την απόδειξη, παρακαλώ.
- ■ Μάλιστα.

Does the waiter amend the bill?

EATING OUT

Try it out

Fill in the blanks

Complete the sentences with the correct word.
a) **πατάτες** b) **νερό** c) **ταβέρνα**
d) **τραπέζι** e) **σουβλάκι**
f) **κρασί**

1 Θέλω ένα ... για δύο.
2 Έχει μια καλή ... εδώ κοντά;
3 Ένα ... με ντομάτα και τζατζίκι.
4 Έχετε κόκκινο ...;
5 Μια μπριζόλα και μια μερίδα ..., παρακαλώ.
6 Ένα ποτήρι ..., παρακαλώ.

As if you were there

Ordering a meal at a Psistariá
☐ **Καλησπέρα σας.**
■ (Say good evening. Ask for one taramosolata, one order of french fries, feta cheese, a salad and one chop)
☐ **Μάλιστα. Τι θα πιείτε;**
■ (A bottle of red wine)
☐ **Δεν έχουμε κόκκινο κρασί.**
■ (A bottle of white wine)
☐ **Εντάξει.**

Sound check

δ (dh) is pronounced like "th" in "this"
επιδόρπιο epidhórpio

θ (th) is pronounced like "th" in "thin"
θέλω thélo

Practice on these words:
λάδι, θαλασσινά, λαδερά, θα

ντομάτας και πιπεριές

83

Menu reader

Courses

Greek meals can go on for some time, but meals revolve around separate dishes rather than separate courses. A typical meal would consist of a selection of *mezédhes* such as *tztatzíki* (garlic, yogurt and cucumber dip), fried zucchini in batter, white haricot beans in tomato sauce, octopus, salad, cheese or spinach pies followed by a meat or fish dish (usually accompanied by just a slice of lemon and perhaps a few fries). If you do not want your dishes together, order them at different times! However, a menu may be divided into *Orektiká* (appetizers), *Entráda* (main meat dishes) and *Glyká*, (dessert). Although a dessert is not a great feature of Greek meals, some places can offer fresh fruit, sometimes Greek yogurt and the odd baked fruit dish in autumn.

Main ways of cooking

βραστός	**vrastós**	boiled
γεμιστός	**yemistós**	stuffed
κοκκινιστός	**kokkinistós**	in a tomato sauce
κρασάτος	**krasátos**	cooked in wine
λεμονάτος	**lemonátos**	in a lemon sauce
μαγειρευτός	**maghireftós**	casseroled
μαρινάτος	**marinátos**	marinaded
στη σούβλα	**sti soúvla**	on the spit
στο φούρνο	**sto foúrno**	baked
σχαριστός	**sharistós**	grilled
τηγανητός	**tighanitós**	fried
ψητός	**psitós**	roast
ωμός	**omós**	raw

The menu

αβοκάντο	**avokádo**	avocado
αγγούρι	**angoúri**	cucumber
αγγουροντομάτα σαλάτα	**angourodomáta saláta**	cucumber and tomato salad
αθερίνα	**atherína**	small whitebait
αλάτι	**aláti**	salt
ανανάς	**ananás**	pineapple
αρακάς	**arakás**	peas
αρνί	**arní**	lamb
αστακός	**astakós**	lobster
αυγά	**avghá**	eggs
αχινός	**ahinós**	sea urchin
αχλάδι	**ahládhi**	pear
βερύκοκκο	**veríkokko**	apricot

MENU READER

βλήτα	vlíta	wild greens
βοδινό	vodhinó	beef
βούτυρο	voútiro	butter
γάλα	ghála	milk
γαλέος	ghaléos	lamprey
γαρίδες	gharídhes	shrimps
γιαούρτι	yiaoúrti	yogurt
γίγαντες γιαχνί	yígantes yiahní	butter beans in tomato sauce
γιουβαρλάκια	yiouvarlákia	meat and rice balls
γιουβέτσι	yiouvétsi	baked Greek pasta
γκρέιπφρουτ	ghréipfrout	grapefruit
γλυκά	ghlíka	sweets
γλυκάδια	ghlikádhia	sweetbread
γλώσσα	ghlósa	sole
γόπες	ghópes	large sardines
γουρουνόπουλο	ghourounópoulo	suckling pig
γραβιέρα	ghraviéra	Greek gruyere
γρανίτα	ghraníta	sorbet
γύρος	yíros	gyros
δαμάσκηνο	dhamáskino	plum
ελιές	eliés	olives
εντρεκότ	endrekót	rib steak
επιδόρπιο	epidhórpio	dessert
εσκαλόπ	eskalóp	cutlet
ζαμπόν	zambón	ham
ζάχαρη	záhari	sugar
ιμάμ μπαϊλντί	imám baildhí	eggplant stuffed with tomatoes
καβούρι	kavoúri	crab
κακαβιά	kakaviá	spicy fish stew
καλαμαράκια	kalamarákia	baby squid
καλαμάρι	kalamári	squid
καλαμπόκι	kalabóki	sweet corn
καπόνι	kapóni	capon
καπνιστός	kapnistós	smoked
καραβήδες	karavídhes	crawfish
καρότα	karótta	carrots
καρπούζι	karpoúzi	watermelon
καρύδι	karídhi	walnut
κασέρι	kaséri	soft yellow cheese
καταΐφι	kataífi	shredded pastry, walnuts and honey
κατεψυγμένος	katepsighménos	frozen
κατσίκι	katsíki	kid
κέικ	keík	cake
κεράσι	kerási	cherry
κέφαλος	kéfalos	mullet
κεφαλοτύρι	kefalotíri	salty yellow cheese
κεφτέδες	keftédhes	meatballs
κοκορέτσι	kokorétsi	grilled sheep's entrails

καλαμάρι

MENU READER

κολοκυθάκια	kolokithákia	zucchini
κομπόστα	kombósta	stewed fruit
κόντρα φιλέτο	kóndra filéto	steak
κοτόπιττα	kotópitta	chicken pie
κοτόπουλο	kotópoulo	chicken
κουκιά	koukiá	broad beans
κουνέλι	kounéli	rabbit
κουνουπίδι	kounoupídhi	cauliflower
κρεατόπιττα	kreatópitta	meat pie
κρεμ καραμελέ	krem karamelé	creme caramel
κρεμμυδάκι	kremidháki	spring onion
κρεμμύδι	kremídhi	onion
κρέπες	krépes	crepes
κυδώνι	kidhóni	quince
κυμάς	kimás	ground beef
κυνήγι	kinighi	game
λαγός	laghós	hare
λάδι	ládhi	oil
λαδολέμονο	ladholémono	oil and lemon dressing
λαδόξυδο	ladhóxidho	oil and vinegar dressing
λακέρδα	lakérdha	salted tuna
λαχανικά	lahaniká	vegetables
λάχανο	láhano	cabbage
λεμόνι	lemóni	lemon
λιθρίνι	lithríni	mullet
λουκάνικο	loukániko	sausage
λουκουμάδες	loukoumádhes	honey fritters
λουκούμι	loukoúmi	Turkish delight
μαγειρίτσα	mayirítsa	easter soup (of lamb's entrails)
μαγιονέζα	mayonéza	mayonnaise
μαιντανός	maidanós	parsley
μακαρόνια	makarónia	spaghetti
μανιτάρια	manitária	mushrooms
μανούρι	manoúri	soft cheese
μανταρίνι	mandaríni	mandarin/tangerine
μαρίδες	marídhes	whitebait
μαρούλι	maroúli	lettuce
μελιτζάνες	melitzánes	eggplant
μελομακάρονο	melomakárono	honey cakes
μερίδα	merídha	portion
μήλο	mílo	apple
μηλόπιττα	milópitta	apple pie
μοσχάρι	moskhári	veal
μους	mous	mousse
μουσακάς	mousakás	mousaka
μουστάρδα	moustárdha	mustard
μπακαλιάρος	bakaliáros	cod
μπακλαβάς	baklavás	flaky pastry with nuts
μπάμιες	bámies	okra
μπανάνα	banána	banana

MENU READER

μπαρμπούνι	barboúni	red mullet
μπαχαρικά	bahariká	spices
μπέικον	béikon	bacon
μπιζέλια	bizélia	peas
μπιντόκ αλα ρους	bidók ala rous	grilled burger with fried egg
μπιφτέκι	biftéki	grilled burger
μπουγάτσα	boughátsa	flaky pastry filled with custard
μπουρεκάκια	bourekákia	small cheese and meat pies with filo pastry
μπούτι	boúti	leg
μπριάμ	briám	kind of ratatouille
μπριζόλες	brizóles	chops
μυαλό	mialó	brain
μύδια	mídhia	mussels
μυζήθρα	mizíthra	white goat's milk cheese
νεράκι	neráki	water
νερό	neró	water
νεφρά	nefrá	kidneys
ντολμάδες	dolmádhes	stuffed grape leaves
ντομάτα	domáta	tomato
ξιφίας	xifías	swordfish
ξύδι	xídhi	vinegar
ομελέτα	omeléta	omelette
ορεκτικά	orektiká	appetizers
παγωμένος	paghoménos	chilled
παγωτό	paghotó	ice-cream
παϊδάκια	paidhákia	lamb chops
παντζάρια	pandzária	beetroot
παπάκι	papáki	duckling
πάπια	pápia	duck
παπουτσάκια	papoutsákia	eggplant dish with bechamel sauce
πάστα	pásta	cake
παστέλι	pastéli	sesame and honey bar
παστουρμάς	pastourmás	spiced cured meat
πατάτες φουρνου	patátes foúrnou	oven-baked potatoes
πατάτες τηγανητές	patátes tighanités	french fries
πατέ	paté	paté
πεπόνι	pepóni	honeydew melon
πέρκα	pérka	perch

ντολμάδες

πιπεριές γεμιστές

MENU READER

πες μελμπά	pes melbá	peach melba
πέστροφα	péstrofa	trout
πιλάφι	piláfi	rice
πιπεριές (γεμιστές)	piperiés (yemistés)	peppers (stuffed)
πλάτη	pláti	shoulder
ποικιλία	pikilía	mixed hors d'oeuvres
πορτοκάλι	portokáli	orange
πουντίγκα	poudínga	pudding
πουρέ	pouré	mashed potato
πρασόρυζο	prasórizo	leeks and rice
πράσα	prása	leeks
ρέγγα	rénga	salted herring
ραδίκια	radhíkia	chicory
ραπανάκια	rapanákia	radishes
ρεβίθια	revíthia	chickpeas
ρόδι	ródhi	pomegranate
ροδάκινο	rodhákino	peach
ρυζόγαλο	rizóghalo	rice pudding
ρώσσικη σαλάτα	róssiki saláta	Russian salad
σαγανάκι	saghanáki	fried cheese
σαλάμι	salámi	salami
σάντουιτς	sándouits	sandwich
σαργός	saryós	sea bream
σαρδέλλα	sardhéla	sardine
σατώμπριάν	satobrián	thick fillet
σέλινο	sélino	celery
σκορδαλιά	skordhaliá	garlic sauce
σκόρδο	skórdho	garlic
σκουμπρί	skoobrí	mackerel
σνίτσελ	snítsel	schnitzel
σούβλα	soúvla	skewer
σούπα	soúpa	soup
σολομός	solomós	salmon
σουπιά	soupiá	cuttlefish
σουτζουκάκια	soudzoukákia	meatballs in sauce
σπανάκι	spanáki	spinach
σπανακόπιττα	spanakópitta	spinach pie
σπανακόρυζο	spanakórizo	spinach and rice
σπαράγγια	sparángia	asparagus
σπετσοφάι	spetsofái	spicy dish of sausage, pepper, etc.
σταφίδα	stafídha	raisin
σταφύλι	stafíli	grape
στιφάδο	stifádho	meat and onion stew
στρείδια	strídhia	oysters
σύκο	síko	fig
συκωτάκια	sikotákia	liver
συναγρίδα	sinagrídha	sea bream
σφυρίδα	sfirídha	grouper (fish)
ταραμοσαλάτα	taramosaláta	fish-roe salad
τζατζίκι	dzadzíki	yogurt, cucumber and garlic salad

MENU READER

τόννος	tónnos	tuna
τοστ	tost	toasted sandwich
τουρσί	toursí	pickle
τούρτα σοκολάτα	toúrta sokoláta	chocolate cake
τριμμένος	trimménos	grated
τσιπούρα	tsipoúra	gilthead bream
τσιπς	tsips	chips
τυρό	tyrí	cheese
τυρόπιττα	tirópitta	cheese pie
φάβα	fáva	split pear pudding
φαγγρί	fangrí	sea bream
φακές	fakés	lentils
φασολάδα	fasoládha	bean soup
φασολάκια	fasolákia	green beans
φασόλια	fasólia	haricot beans
φασόλια γιαχνί	fasólia yahní	beans in tomato sauce
φέτα	féta	ewe's milk cheese
φιλέτο	filéto	fillet
φουντούκι	foundoúki	hazelnut
φράουλες	fráoules	strawberries
φρικασέ	frikasé	fricassee
φρούτα	froúta	fruit
χαβιάρι	haviári	caviar
χαλβάς	halvás	sweetmeat with chopped almonds and honey
χάμπουργκερ	hámbourger	hamburger
χέλι	héli	eel
χόρτα	hórta	wild greens
χουρμάς	hourmás	date
χταπόδι	htapódhi	octopus
χυλοπίτες	hilopítes	square-shaped pasta
χωριάτικη σαλάτα	horiátiki saláta	mixed "Greek" salad
ψαρόσουπα	psarósoupa	fish soup
ψωμάκι	psomáki	(piece of) bread, roll
ψωμί	psomí	bread

For drinks see Café Life, p72–73.

χωριάτικη σαλάτα

Entertainment and leisure

Finding events

■ English language newspapers. The *Athens News* is a daily national newspaper, listing events, movies, and TV programs.

■ There is also a weekly listings magazine for Athens and Piraeus, *Athinórama*, a mine of information even for those with minimal Greek, as is its rival *Downtown*. There is a modest equivalent in English, *Athenscope*.

■ Offices of EOT, the national tourist organization, which can be found in main towns and resorts. These can supply maps and local pamphlets with ideas of what to see and do.

❗ What is there to see here?
Τι έχει να δούμε εδώ;
● Ti éhi na dhoúme edhó?

Participation events

Sports

■ **Watersports** Windsurfing can be done at almost any resort or island around the country. For beginners, a few lessons make all the difference: these are widely available, as is board rental. Waterskiing is almost as easy to find. Other common watersports are snorkeling, parasailing and scuba diving, the latter limited to certain resorts such as Mykonos, or in Glyfáda, just south of Athens.

■ **Golf courses** exist in Corfu, Halkidikí, Rhodes and near Athens.

■ **Yachting** buffs have the option of sailing themselves around the Greek seas or having a captain do it for them. Captains and yachts can be rented (further information from EOT) and for a group are not such an expensive option. There are marinas around the country, such as at Glyfáda, Varkiza and Vouliagmeni near Athens; Zéa and Paleó Pháliron in Pireus; and those in Corfu, Halkidikí, Pátras, Thessaloníki and Rhodes.

■ **Skiing** Though most visitors associate Greece with the islands and the sea, you can also ski here on some of the most reasonably priced ski slopes in Europe. Snow, however, cannot be guaranteed. The most popular destination for skiers, between December and April, is Mount Parnassós, near Delphi. On winter weekends the town of Aráchova takes on an aprés-ski ambience, with trendy bars and upscale tavernas lively on Saturday nights. Other organized ski centers around the country include: Helmós, Kalávrita in the Peloponnese; Velouhi in Karpeníssi, Central Greece; Hánia in the Pelion; Mount Falakrón near Dráma and Pisodhéri near Flórina, both in Macedonia.

■ **Hiking** A highly recommended way to see parts of the country not covered by package deal operators is to join hikes or walks organized by Trekking Hellas (Athens. Tel: 01 325 0317/325 0853). From March

ENTERTAINMENT AND LEISURE

Spectator events

■ **Soccer and basketball** The Greeks never seem to get enough of these on television, and bars can be highly charged when there is a big match on. For live football, the big teams are Panathanáikos and AEK in Athens, Olympiákos in Piraeus and PAOK of Thessaloníki, though most regional towns have their own teams. Basketball is hugely popular, as is volleyball.

■ **Movies and theater** Most main towns have several movie theaters showing films in their original version. In summer, open-air theaters are prevalent, an experience not to be missed. Though your Greek may not be up to all performances, it is worth attending the plays performed in Greece's classical theaters such as in Epidaurus and Athens.

■ **Music and dance** Tourist resorts have made "traditional Greek dancing" something of a cliché, but in fact Greek music remains extremely popular with the young and old alike. Try and visit a club specializing in Rembétika, one of the most evocative strands of Greek music. For details of festivals specializing in song and dance, see p26–27.

Do you have a map of the town?
Έχετε ένα σχέδιο της πόλης;
Éhete éna skhédhio tis pólis?

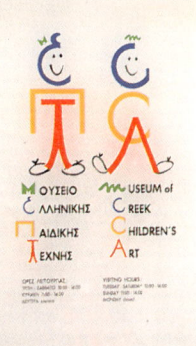

through to November they run hikes of varying length and ease over hill and mountain country on the mainland and some islands. Most of inland Greece and the Greek islands themselves offer plenty to walkers of any ability. Try and stick to established footpaths and get a good map, as some of Greece is extremely mountainous and remote; take care in gorges, which can become flooded without warning outside summer.

Children

Children are held in high esteem in Greece and they are welcome everywhere. That said, there are not many places designed purely for children. If beaches become boring, however, one exception is the Children's Museum in the Plaka, Athens, where special activities are offered.

Children's playgrounds are found in almost every neighborhood around the country. However, facilities within shopping areas and restaurants are nonexistent, so for those with very young children it can be difficult when they need changing or bottles warmed.

Palace of the Grand Masters, Rhodes

ENTERTAINMENT AND LEISURE

Phrasemaker

Getting to know the place

Do you have (a map of the town/an entertainment guide)?	Έχετε (ένα σχέδιο της πόλης/έναν οδηγό διασκέδασης);	Éhete (éna shédhio tis pólis/énan odhighó dhiaskédhasis)?
Do you have any information in English?	Έχετε πληροφορίες στα Αγγλικά;	Éhete plirofories sta Angliká?
What is there to (see/do here)?	Τί έχει να (δούμε/κάνουμε) εδώ;	Ti éhi na (dhoúme/kánoume) edhó?
Is there (a guided tour/a bus tour)?	Υπάρχει ξενάγηση (με ξεναγό/με λεωφορείο);	Ipárhi xenáyisi (me xenaghó/me leoforío)?
Is there a (movie theater/night club) here?	Υπάρχει (σινεμά/κλαμπ) εδώ;	Ipárhei (sinemá/club) edhó?
Can you recommend a restaurant?	Μπορείτε να μας συστήσετε ένα εστιατόριο;	Boríte na mas sistísete éna estiatório?
Is there anything for the children to do?	Υπάρχει κάτι να κάνουν τα παιδιά;	Ipárhi káti na kánoun ta edhiá?

Τί σας ενδιαφέρει;
Tí sas endhiaféri?   What are you interested in?

Things to do or see

beach	η παραλία	i paralía
castle	το κάστρο	to kástro
concert	η συναυλία	i sinavlía
disco	η ντίσκο	i disco
festival	το φεστιβάλ	to festivál
fireworks	τα πυροτεχνήματα	ta pyrotehnímata
gallery	η πινακοθήκη	i pinakothíki
movie theater	ο κινηματογράφος/το σινεμά	o kinimatoghráfos/to sinemá

ENTERTAINMENT AND LEISURE

museum	το μουσείο	to mousío
nightclub	το κέντρο/κλαμπ	to kéndro/club
race track	ο ιππόδρομος	o ipódhromos
show	το πρόγραμμα/καμπαρέ	to prógrama/cabaret
stadium	το στάδιο/γήπεδο	to stádhio/yípedho
theater	το θέατρο	to théatro

Getting more information

Where is the (swimming pool/concert hall)?	Πού είναι η (πισίνα/αίθουσα συναυλιών); Poú íne i (pisína/éthousa sinavlión)?
Where does the tour start?	Πού αρχίζει η ξενάγηση; Poú arhízi i xenáyisi?
What time does it (start/end)?	Τι ώρα (αρχίζει/τελειώνει); Tí óra (arhízi/telióni)?
What time does it (open/close)?	Τι ώρα (ανοίγει/κλείνει); Tí óra (aníghi/klíni)?
Do you need tickets?	Χρειάζονται εισιτήρια; Hriázonde isitíria?
Where can I buy tickets?	Πού μπορώ να αγοράσω εισιτήρια; Poú boró na aghoráso isitíria?

Δεν χρειάζεστε εισιτήρια. Dhen hriázeste isitíria.	You don't need tickets.
Συγγνώμη, τελείωσαν. Sighnómi, telíosan.	Sorry, it's sold out.
Στην κεντρική πλατεία, στις 10 η ώρα. Stin kendrikí platía, stis 10 i óra.	In the main square, at 10 o'clock.
9.30 με 7.00 μμ. 9.30 me 7.00 mm.	From 9:30 to 7:00 pm.
Στο εκδοτήριο. Sto ekdhotírio.	At the ticket office.
Ορίστε στον (χάρτη/σχέδιο). Oríste ston (hárti/shédhio).	Here on the (map/plan).

ENTERTAINMENT AND LEISURE

Getting in

Do you have any tickets?	Έχετε εισιτήρια;	Éhete isitíria?
How much (is it/are they)?	Πόσο (κάνει/κάνουν);	Póso (káni/kanoun)?
Two tickets, please.	Δύο εισιτήρια, παρακαλώ.	Dhío isitíria, parakaló.
For (Saturday/tomorrow).	Για (το Σάββατο/αύριο).	Ya (to Sávato/ávrio).
Are there any concessions?	Υπάρχει κάποια έκπτωση;	Ipárhi kápia ékptosi?
How long does it last?	Πόση ώρα κρατάει;	Pósi óra kratái?
Does the film have subtitles?	Το έργο έχει υποτίτλους;	To érgho éhi ipotítlous?
Is there a program?	Υπάρχει πρόγραμμα;	Ipárhi próghrama?
Is this seat taken?	Αυτή η θέση είναι πιασμένη;	Aftí i thési íne piasméni?
Is there an intermission?	Υπάρχει διάλειμμα;	Ipárhi dhiálima?

Ναι, για (φοιτητές/παιδιά/συνταξιούχους).	Ne, ya (fitités/pedhiá/sindaxioúhous).	Yes, for (students/children/senior citizens).
Ένα διάλειμμα είκοσι λεπτών.	Éna dhiálima íkosi leptón.	One intermission of twenty minutes.
Είναι (ελεύθερη/πιασμένη).	Íne (eléftheri/piasméni).	It's (free/taken).

Αρχαιολογικό Μουσείο / Archaeological Museum

Signs

Αντρών	Andrón	Men
Μπαρ	Bar	Bar
Πλατεία	Platía	Orchestra (seat)
Έξοδος	Éxodhos	Exit
Εξώστης	Exóstis	Gallery
Εξώστης δεύτερος	Exóstis dhéfteros	Balcony
Γκαρνταρόμπα	Gardaróba	Cloakroom
Σκάλα	Skála	Stairs
Θεωρείο	Theorío	Box
Τουαλέτες	Toualétes	Restroom
Γυναικών	Yinekón	Ladies

ΝΑΥΤΙΚΟ ΜΟΥΣΕΙΟ ΤΗΣ ΕΛΛΑΔΟΣ / HELLENIC MARITIME MUSEUM

ENTERTAINMENT AND LEISURE

Swimming and sunbathing

Can I use the hotel pool?	Μπορώ να χρησιμοποιήσω την πισίνα του ξενοδοχείου; Boró na hrisimopííso tin pisína tou xenodhohíou?
Where are the (locker rooms/showers)?	Πού είναι τα (αποδυτήρια/ντους); Poú íne ta (apodhitíria/dous)?
I'd like to rent a(n) (umbrella/towel).	Θα ήθελα να νοικιάσω μια (ομπρέλα/πετσέτα). Tha íthela na nikiáso mia (ombréla/petséta).

On the beach

deck chair	η σεζλόγκ	i sezlóng
towel	η πετσέτα	i petséta
sunglasses	τα γυαλιά ηλίου	ta yialiá ilíou
sun lounger	η ξαπλώστρα	i xaplóstra
suntan lotion	η κρέμα ηλίου	i créma ilíou
table	το τραπέζι	to trapézi
umbrella	η ομπρέλα	i ombréla

Sports facilities

Where can I (go swimming/play tennis/watch basketball)?	Πού μπορώ να (πάω για μπάνιο/παίξω τένις/δω μπάσκετ); Poú boró na (páo ya bánio/péxo ténis/dho básket)?
I'd like to rent (a racket/waterskis).	Θα ήθελα να νοικιάσω (μια ρακέτα/θαλάσσιο σκι). Tha íthela na nikiáso (mia rakéta/thalásio ski).
I'd like to take (skiing/sailing) lessons.	Θα ήθελα να κάνω μαθήματα (σκι/ιστιοπλοΐας). Tha íthela na káno mathímata (ski/istioploías).

Paleokastritsa, Corfu

ENTERTAINMENT AND LEISURE

Sports

climbing	η ορειβασία	i orivasía
football	το ποδόσφαιρο	to podhósfero
golf	το γκολφ	to golf
sailing	η ιστιοπλοΐα	i istioploía
skiing	το σκι	to ski
surfing	το σέρφιγκ	to sérfing
tennis	το τένις	to ténis
volleyball	το βόλεϋ	to vóley
walking	το περπάτημα	to perpátima
water ski	το θαλάσσιο σκι	to thalásio ski
wind surfing	το σέρφιγκ	to sérfing

Sports equipment

boat	το σκάφος	to skáfos
boots	οι μπότες	i bótes
dinghy/sailboat	το καΐκι	to kaíki
golf clubs	τα μπαστούνια	ta bastoúnia
life jacket	το σωσίβιο	to sosívio
(rubber) dinghy	η λαστιχένια βάρκα	i lastihénia várka
skis	τα σκι	ta ski
tennis racket/ balls	η ρακέτα του τένις/μπάλλες	i rakéta tou ténis/báles
water skis	τα θαλάσσια σκι	ta thalásia ski
(wind) surfboard	το σερφ	to serf

ENTERTAINMENT AND LEISURE

Language works

Getting information

1 Asking about a guided tour.
- ■ Υπάρχει ξενάγηση με ξεναγό;
- □ Μάλιστα.
- ■ Τί ώρα αρχίζει;
- □ Στις δώδεκα.
- ■ Πού μπορώ να αγοράσω εισιτήρια;
- □ Στο εκδοτήριο.

The tour starts at . . . and you get tickets from . . .

Getting in

2 Booking concert seats
- ■ Πότε είναι η συναυλία παρακαλώ;
- □ Την Τετάρτη.
- ■ Έχει εισιτήρια;
- □ Μάλιστα.
- ■ Πόσο κάνουν;
- □ Δύο χιλιάδες δραχμές.

Which day does the concert take place? How much are tickets?

Sport

3 Asking about playing tennis.
- ■ Γειά σας. Τί ώρα μπορώ να παίξω τένις;
- □ Στις τέσσερις ή στις έξι.
- ■ Στις έξι. Θέλω να νοικιάσω δύο ρακέτες.
- □ Μάλιστα. Χίλιες πεντακόσιες δραχμές.

What times are available?

Try it out

Jumbled words

The following words for places have been jumbled. Put the letters in the correct order.
eg οεμίσυο = μουσείο
1 θινήκκπηαο
2 ορτθέα
3 αρπαλία
4 σίιπνα
5 σκίοντ

As if you were there

Asking about a nightclub
- □ (Ask what time the nightclub opens)
- ■ Στις εννιά.
- □ (Ask what time the show starts)
- ■ Στις δώδεκα.
- □ (Ask if you need tickets)
- ■ Δεν χρειάζεστε.
- □ (Say thank you)

Sound check

η, ι, υ, οι, ει These five vowels, or combinations of vowels, all produce the same sound "i" like "ee" in "feet."
πόλη póli
τι ti
υπάρχει ipárhi
νοικιάσω nikiáso
έχει éhi

Practice on these words:
αρχίζει, ξενάγηση, δύο, εισιτήρια, συστήσετε

Emergencies

Crime

Compared to much of Europe, crime rates in Greece remain comfortably low. Even in Athens, women should feel markedly safer than in many capitals, though the Omónia Square area is best avoided after dark.

police

Greeks are particularly honest when it comes to personal belongings and it is usual for them to leave things unattended on beaches, at cafés, etc. However, it is better not to tempt fate as thefts in tourist areas may occur. If you do have anything stolen or need the police, go to the *astinomikó tmíma* (the local police station) or contact the tourist police, who are more likely to speak languages other than Greek.

The most common source of complaints stems from taxi drivers, who are infamous for over-charging; passsengers from airports are notoriously vulnerable. Look for a list of approximate rates before leaving the arrivals terminal or ask the police officer on duty before taking your taxi. If you feel there is a serious problem, tell the driver to drive to the nearest police station *(astinomikó tmíma)*. This is normally enough to settle the issue.

- Can you help me?
- Μπορείτε να με βοηθήσετε;
- Boríte na me voithísete?

Health

The single biggest enemy to your health in Greece is the country's number one attraction, the sun. Never underestimate its strength.
- Rent (or buy) a sun umbrella and avoid sunbathing during the middle of the day.
- Tap water is generally good, though on some islands (such as Santoríni) the water is saline. If you are unsure, bottled water is available everywhere.
- Stomach upsets can be common. Pharmacists can help you with everyday medical problems and most medicines can be issued without the need for a prescription.
- Every town has one pharmacy open for emergencies; this information is posted on its doors.

EMERGENCIES

Hospitals

Most regions have a local state hospital though not all have a great reputation. In larger cities on the mainland, there are private hospitals that offer faster and more reliable treatment. These can be found listed in the **Χρυσος Οδηγός** *Hrisos Odhiyos* (Yellow Pages) or try consulting the tourist police to see if they can help you locate the nearest one. Before traveling to Greece, check to see what exactly your travel insurance policy covers you for.

> **!** Is there someone here who speaks English?
> **●** Υπάρχει κανένας εδώ που μιλάει Αγγλικά;
> Ipárhi kanénas edhó pou milái Angliká?

Wildlife

The only venomous snakes in Greece are the adder and a related species, but they are not found in abundance. Scorpions are even rarer, but are poisonous. If you are worried about these, a special device to treat the sting immediately is available from good Greek pharmacies. In the unlikely event of being bitten or stung, medical help should be sought without delay.

Jellyfish and sea urchins are a minor hazard when swimming. For mosquitoes, you can buy a small electrical device to ensure your night's sleep is uninterrupted. This is available from supermarkets and pharmacies.

Restrooms

These have improved considerably in recent years. In the cities public conveniences are normally clean. Look for **Ανδρών/ΑΝΔΡΩΝ** for men and **Γυναικών/ΓΥΝΑΙΚΩΝ** for women. Elsewhere, the facilities at restaurants and cafés may be used. Regrettably, disabled people are barely accommodated.

Post offices

These open on Monday–Friday from 7:30 am to 1:30 or 2:00 pm and are usually crowded. Stamps *(gramatóssima)* are cheaper from post offices, but can also be bought from stands *(periptero)*. Mail letters in the yellow mailboxes; some have a separate slot marked *exterikó* for overseas mail.

Public telephones

Phones are plentiful; almost all require cards *(tilekárta)* which are available from stands, mini-markets and Telephone Company (OTE) offices. At stands (see Buying things p58) there are public phones with meters and you will be charged accordingly at the end of your call. The OTE offices are useful for long-distance calls, especially if you do not want to be limited by a card. They can be found in all towns and many villages. Hotels charge rates well above the norm, so use outside phones to keep your bills down.

99

EMERGENCIES

Useful telephone numbers

Codes
Athens 01
Thessaloníki 031.

Directory assistance
131 for Athens, Piráeus and Attiki
132 for the provinces
161 for international calls.

Emergencies
Police: 100 (to report serious matters)
Ambulance: 166
Fire: 199
Tourist Police: 171 (for minor tourist-related problems or advice in English, Greek, German and French)

Additional emergency services – Athens
Poisoning Treatment Center: 779 3777
SOS Medicins, 24-hour Private Medical Service: 322 0015/0046.
Holiday and Night Duty Doctors (2pm – 7am): 105
Holiday and Night Duty Hospitals: 106

Embassies and consulates
- **USA** 91 Vassilissis Sofias
  (01) 721 2951
  59 Nikis, Thessaloniki
  (031) 266 121
- **Canada** 4 Ioannou Genadiou
  (01) 725 4011
- **Ireland** 7 Vassileos Constantiou
  (01) 723 2771
- **New Zealand** 24 Xenias
  (01) 771 0112
- **South Africa** 60 Kifissias
  (01) 680 6645
- **UK** 1 Ploutarchou and Ipsilantou
  (01) 7223 6211
  8 Venizelou, Thessaloniki
  (031) 278 006
- **Australia** 37 Dimitriou Soustou
  (01) 644 7303

Phrasemaker

General

Help!	Βοήθεια!
	Voíthia!
Excuse me/Hello there! (to attract attention)	Συγνώμη!
	Sighnómi!
Thank you.	Ευχαριστώ.
	Efharistó.
Can you help me?	Μπορείτε να με βοηθήσετε;
	Boríte na me voithísete?
Where is the nearest (police station/hospital)?	Πού είναι το πιο κοντινό (τμήμα/νοσοκομείο);
	Poú ine to pio kondinó (tmíma/nosokomío)?
Leave me alone.	Αφήστε με ήσυχη.
	Afíste me ísihi.
I'll call the police.	Θα φωνάξω την αστυνομία.
	Tha fonáxo tin astinomía.

dentist

NIK.
KPHTIKOΣ
ΧΕΙΡΟΥΡΓΟΣ
ΟΔΟΝΤΙΑΤΡΟΣ

ΙΑΤΡΕΙΟΝ

doctor

Health

I need (a doctor/an ambulance).	Χρειάζομαι (γιατρό/ασθενοφόρο).
	Hriázome (yiatró/asthenofóro).
It's urgent.	Είναι επείγον.
	ine epígon.
Is there someone here who speaks English?	Υπάρχει κανένας εδώ πού μιλάει Αγγλικά;
	Ipárhi kanénas edhó poú milái Angliká?
I'd like an appointment with a (doctor/dentist).	Θέλω να κλείσω ραντεβού με τον (γιατρό/ οδοντογιατρό).
	Thélo na klíso randevú me ton (yiatró/odhondoyiatró).

EMERGENCIES

Parts of the body

ankle	ο αστράγαλος	o astrághalos
arm	το χέρι	to héri
back	η πλάτη	i pláti
chest	το στήθος	to stíthos
(inner/outer) ear	το (εσωτερικό/ εξωτερικό) αυτί	to (esoterikó/ exoterikó) afti
elbow	ο αγκώνας	o agónas
eye (eyes)	το μάτι (μάτια)	to máti (mátia)
finger	το δάχτυλο	to dháhtilo
foot	το πόδι	to pódhi
hand (hands)	το χέρι (χέρια)	to héri (héria)
head	το κεφάλι	to kefáli
heart	η καρδιά	i kardhiá
hip	ο γοφός	o ghofós
kidneys	τα νεφρά	ta nefrá
knee	το γόνατο	to ghónato
leg (legs)	το πόδι (πόδια)	to pódhi (pódhia)
liver	το συκώτι	to sikóti
neck	ο λαιμός	o lemós
nose	η μύτη	i míti
toe (toes)	το δάχτυλο (δάχτυλα)	to dháhtilo (dháhtila)
shoulder	ο ώμος	o ómos
stomach	το στομάχι	to stomáhi
throat	ο λαιμός	o lemós
tooth (teeth)	το/τα δόντι (δόντια)	to/ta dhóndi (dhóndia)

the Acropolis, Athens

EMERGENCIES

Telling the doctor

My stomach hurts.	Πονάει το στομάχι μου. Ponái to stomáhi mou.
My eyes hurt.	Πονάνε τα μάτια μου. Ponáne ta mátia mou.
It hurts here.	Πονάει εδώ. Ponái edhó.
(My son/My daughter) has a temperature.	(Ο γιός/η κόρη) μου έχει πυρετό. (O yiós/i kóri) mou éhi piretó.
She/He feels sick.	Έχει ναυτία. Éhi naftía.

Common symptoms

I have diarrhea.	Έχω διάρροια. Ého dhiária.
I have constipation.	Έχω δυσκοιλιότητα. Ého dhiskiliótita.
I have a sore throat.	Έχω το λαιμό μου. Ého to lemó mou.
I have a cough.	Έχω βήχα. Ého víha.
I have (a headache/hay fever).	Έχω (πονοκέφαλο/αλλεργικό συνάχι). Ého (ponokéfalo/allerghikó sináhi).
I have a cold.	Είμαι κρυωμέν(ος/η). Íme kriomén(os/i).
I have vomited.	Έκανα έμετο. Ékana émeto.
I can't (move/breathe).	Δεν μπορώ να (κουνηθώ/αναπνεύσω). Dhen boró na (kounithó/anapnéfso).

(See p109 for information on the different forms for men and women)

Common accidents

I've cut myself.	Κόπηκα. Kópika.
I've burnt myself.	Κάηκα. Káika.
I've been stung by an insect.	Με τσίμπισε έντομο. Me tsíbise éndomo.
I've been bitten by a dog.	Με δάγκωσε σκύλος. Me dhágose skílos.

Special problems

I'm allergic to (animals/antibiotics).	Έχω αλλεργία στα (ζώα/αντιβιοτικά). **Ého alleryia sta (zóa/andiviotiká).**
I am (diabetic/pregnant).	Είμαι (διαβητικός/ή/έγκυος). **Íme (dhiavitikós/í/éngios).**
I have a toothache.	Έχω πονόδοντο. **Ého ponódhondo.**
I've lost a filling.	Μου έπεσε ένα σφράγισμα. **Mou épese éna sfráyisma.**
Δεν είναι σοβαρό. **Dhen ine sovaró.**	It's not serious.
Το κόκκαλο είναι σπασμένο. **To kókkalo ine spasméno.**	The bone is broken.
Θα χρειαστείτε εγχείρηση. **Tha hriastíte enhírisi.**	You will need an operation.
Ορίστε η συνταγή. **Oríste i sintayí.**	This is a prescription.
Θα σας βάλω ένα (προσωρινό) σφράγισμα. **Tha sas válo éna (prosorinó) sfráyisma.**	I'll put in a (temporary) filling.
Πρέπει να βγάλω αυτό το δόντι. **Prépi na vghálo aftó to dhónti.**	I'll have to take this tooth out.

EMERGENCIES

At the pharmacy

Do you have something for . . .	Έχετε κάτι για . . . Éhete káti ya . . .
a cold/cough/ diarrhea	κρυολόγημα/το βήχα/ τι διάρροια kriológhima/to víha/ti dhiária
sunburn/constipation	έγκαυμα από τον ήλιο/ δυσκοιλιότητα égavma apó ton ílio/ dhiskiliótita
burns/insect stings	εγκαύματα/τσιμπήματα egávmata/tsibímata
Do you have any . . .	Έχετε . . . Éhete . . .
adhesive bandages	χανζαπλάστ hanzaplást
after-sun lotion	γαλάκτωμα μετά τον ήλιο ghaláktoma metá ton ílio
antihistamine	αντισταμινικό andistaminikó
aspirin	ασπιρίνες aspirínes
baby food	βρεφική τροφή vrefikí trofí
contact lens solution	υγρό φακών επαφής ighró fakón epafís
condom	προφυλακτικό profilaktikó
cough syrup	σιρόπι για το βήχα sirópi yia to víha

(Πάρτε/Βάλτε) . . . (Párte/Válte) . . .	(Take/Apply) . . .
. . . αυτό το φάρμακο/αυτή την αλοιφή/αυτή την κρέμα . . . aftó to fármako/aftí tin alifí /aftí tin kréma	. . . this (medicine/lotion/cream)
. . . αυτά τα χάπια / αυτά τα αντιβιοτικά . . . aftá ta hápia/aftá ta antiviotiká	. . . these (pills/antibiotics)
. . . (μια φορά/δύο φορές/τρεις φορές) την ημέρα . . . . . . (mia forá/dhío forés/treis fores) tin iméra . . .	. . . (once/twice/three times) a day . . .
(πριν/μετά) το φαγητό (prin/metá) to fayitó	(before/after) meals
με νερό me neró	with water

EMERGENCIES

Μασήστε, μην (δαγκώνετε/ καταπίνετε). Masíste, min (dhangónete/ katapínete).	Chew, don't (bite/swallow).
Πρέπει να (αναπαυθείτε/ κοιμηθείτε). Prépi na (anapafthíte/ kimithíte).	You must (rest/sleep).

πετρελαιο — diesel

Car breakdown

I've broken down.	Το αυτοκίνητό μου χάλασε. To aftokínitó mou hálase.	
on the Athens – Thessaloniki highway	στην Εθνική οδό Αθήνα – Θεσσαλονίκη stin Ethnikí odhó Athens – Thessaloníki	
X kilometers from Y	X χιλιόμετρα από Y X hiliómetra apó Y	
The (engine/steering) isn't working.	(Η μηχανή/Το τιμόνι) δεν δουλεύει. (I mihaní/To timóni) dhen dhoulévi.	
The brakes aren't working.	Τα φρένα δεν δουλεύουν. Ta fréna den dhoulévoun.	
I have a flat tire.	Έμεινα από λάστιχο. Émina apó lástiho.	
I've run out of gas.	Έμεινα απο βενζίνα. Émina apó venzína.	
When will it be ready?	Πότε θα είναι έτοιμο; Póte tha íne étimo?	
passport number	αριθμός διαβατηρίου arithmós dhiavatiríou	

Car parts

accelerator	το γκάζι	to gázi
battery	η μπαταρία	i bataría
brakes	τα φρένα	ta fréna
clutch	το χειρόφρενο	to hirófreno
engine	η μηχανή	i mihaní
gears	οι ταχύτητες	i tahítites
lights	τα φώτα	ta fóta
radiator	το ψυγείο	to psiyio
steering wheel	το τιμόνι	to timóni
tires	τα λάστιχα	ta lástiha
wheels	οι ρόδες	i ródhes
windshield wiper	ο καθαριστήρας	o katharistíras

EMERGENCIES

Theft or loss

I've lost my (wallet/passport).	Έχασα το (πορτοφόλι/ διαβατήριό) μου.	Éhasa to (portofóli/ dhiavatírió) mou.
I've had my (watch/ bag) stolen.	Μου έκλεψαν (το ρολόι/τρν τσάντα) μου.	Mou éklepsan (to rolói mou/tin tsánda) mou.
In (the street/ a store).	(Στο δρόμο/Σ'ένα μαγαζί).	(Sto dhrómo/S'éna maghazí).

Valuables

briefcase	ο χαρτοφύλακας	o hartofílakas
camera	η (φωτογραφική) μηχανή	i (fotoghrafikí) mihaní
car	το αυτοκίνητο	to aftokínito
credit card	η πιστωτική κάρτα	i pistotikí kárta
driver's license	το δίπλωμα οδήγησης	to dhíploma odhíyisis
handbag	η τσάντα	i tsánda
jewelry	τα κοσμήματα	ta kosmímata
money	τα λεφτά	ta leftá
necklace	το κολλιέ	to kollié
passport	το διαβατήριο	to dhiavatírio
purse	το πορτοφόλι	to portofóli
suitcase	η βαλίτσα	i valítsa
tickets	τα εισιτήρια	ta isitíria
wallet	το πορτοφόλι	to portofóli

Τι έγινε;	Ti éghine?	What happened?
Πότε...;	Póte...?	When...?
Πως λέγεστε;	Pos léyeste?	What is your name?
Πού...;	Roú...?	Where...?

Ποιά είναι η διεύθυνση σας; Poiá ine í dhiéfthinsi sas?	What is your address?
Πού μένετε; Roú ménete?	Where are you staying?
αριθμός κυκλοφορίας arithmós kikloforías	license plate number
Συμπληρώστε αυτό το έντυπο. Sibliróste aftó to éndipo.	Fill out this form.
Ελάτε αργότερα. Eláte arghótera.	Come back later.

107

EMERGENCIES

Language works

At the pharmacy

1 You are suffering from diarrhea.
□ Έχετε κάτι για τη διάρροια;
■ Πάρτε αυτά τα χάπια. Τρεις φορές την ημέρα.
□ Πότε;
■ Πριν το φαγητό.

How often do you have to take the tablets?

ΕΛΛΗΝΙΚΗ ΑΣΤΥΝΟΜΙΑ
ΑΣΤΥΝΟΜΙΚΟ ΤΜΗΜΑ ΠΑΡΟΥ
POLICE

Theft or loss

2 Reporting the loss of your camera at the police station.
□ Έχασα τη μηχανή μου.
■ Πού;
□ Στο ξενοδοχείο μου.
■ Πού μένετε;
□ Στο ξενοδοχείο Αύρα.
■ Συμπληρώστε αυτό το έντυπο.

(ξενοδοχείο = hotel)

What are you asked to do?

Breakdown

3 Your rented car breaks down.
□ Το αυτοκίνητο μου χάλασε.
■ Πού είσαστε;
□ Στην Εθνική οδό Αθήνα-Θεσσαλονίκη.
■ Ερχόμαστε.
□ Πόση ώρα θα κάνετε;
■ Μισή ώρα.

(ερχόμαστε = we're coming)

It will take them an hour to come to your rescue: true/false?

Try it out

Making connections

Match the two halves of the words to make six things you might lose on holiday.
τσα + ντα = τσάντα
τσα   φόλι
βαλι   τήριο
πορτο φτά
διαβα ντα
μηχ   τσα
λε   ανή

As if you were there

Buying cream for sunburn and after-sun lotion at the pharmacy.

□ (Say good morning)
■ Καλημέρα.
□ (Ask if they have got something for sunburn)
■ Βάλτε αυτή την κρέμα τρείς φορές την ημέρα.
□ (And after-sun lotion)
■ Ορίστε.
□ (Ask how much it is altogether)

Sound check

γ can be pronounced in a number of ways depending on the letter that follows:
γόνατο ghonato
γιατρός yiatros
Αγγλικά anglika
δάγκωσε dhagose

Practice on these words:
για, αγκώνας, συγγνώμη, σαγόνι

Language builder

Using the words and phrases in this book will enable you to deal with most everyday situations. If you want to go a bit further and start building your own phrases, there are a few rules about Greek which will help you.

Gender

All nouns in Greek are feminine, masculine or neuter. As you go along you'll probably recognize that most words ending in **-ος, -ας, -ης** are masculine; those ending in **-α, -η** are feminine; those ending in **-ο, -ι, -α** are neuter.
The word's gender affects: a) the form of "a" and "the" used with it; b) the form of adjectives used with it.

"a" and "the": the articles

"a"
Feminine: **μία (mía)**
Μία εφημερίδα (a newspaper)
mía efimerídha

μία μπύρα (a beer)
mía byra

Masculine: **ένας (énas)**
ένας δρόμος (a road)
énas dhrómos

ένας μουσακάς (a mousaka)
énas mousakás

Neuter: **ένα (éna)**
ένα περιοδικό (a magazine)
éna periodhikó

ένα σουπερμάρκετ
(a supermarket)
éna soupermárket

"the"
When you are referring to just one thing or person, you use **η** for feminine words, **ο** for masculine and **το** for neuter. If there is more than one thing or person, as in "the shirts" or "the dresses," you use **οι** for feminine and masculine words and **τα** for neuter.

Feminine
Singular: **η (i)** Plural: **οι (i)**
η φούστα (the skirt) οι φούστες
i foústa i foústes

Masculine
Singular: **ο (ï)** Plural: **οι (i)**
ο όροφος (the floor) οι όροφοι
o órofos i órofi

Neuter
Singular: **το (to)** Plural: **τα (ta)**
το φουστάνι (the dress) τα φουστάνια
to foustáni ta foustánia

Singular and plural

When you talk about more than one person or thing, you need to change the ending of the noun:

Feminine words
-α changes to -ες
μία μπύρα δύο μπύρες
(beer)
mía býra dhío býres

-η changes to -ες
μία επιταγή δύο επιταγές
(check)
mía epitayí dhío epitayés

Masculine words
-ος changes to -οι
ένας κύριος δύο κύριοι
(gentleman)
énas kýrios dhío kýrioi

LANGUAGE BUILDER

-ης changes to -ες
ένας χάρτης δύο χάρτες
(map)
énas hártis dhío hártes

-ας changes to -ες
ένας άντρας δύο άντρες
(man)
énas ándras dhío ándres

Neuter nouns
-ο changes to -α
ένα τσιγάρο δύο τσιγάρα
(cigarette)
éna tsigháro dhío tsighára

-α changes to -ατα
ένα γράμμα δύο γράμματα
(letter)
éna ghráma dhío ghrámata

-ι changes to -ια
ένα πεπόνι δύο πεπόνια
(melon)
éna pepóni dhío pepónia

Note: If you're ordering something that is masculine, you will need to use a different form of the noun - taking off the ς from the end of the word. (In the plural, the only change is to words ending in -οι, which change to -ους.) Feminine and neuter words remain unchanged.

ένα κατάλογο παρακαλώ
a menu please
éna katálogho parakaló

δύο καταλόγους παρακαλώ
two menus please
dhío katalóghous parakaló

The words for "You"

The general rule is that **εσείς** is used for strangers or more than one person and **εσύ** is for a friend or when talking to one person. It is most sensible at first to use **εσείς (esís)**, since you will normally be speaking to someone you don't know too well. The word you use will often affect the form of the verb that follows.

Verbs

Verbs, which are usually actions, change their endings quite often in Greek. The things that make the endings change are:
– who is doing the action (the person)
– how many of them there are (singular/ plural)
– when they did or are doing it

Πόσο κάνει το πεπόνι;
Póso káni to pepóni?
How much does the melon cost?

Πόσο κάνουν τα πεπόνια;
Póso kánoun ta pepónia?
How much do the melons cost?

Μιλάω ελληνικά.
Miláo eliniká.
I speak Greek.

Η κόρη μου μιλάει ελληνικά.
I kóri mou milái eliniká.
My daughter speaks Greek.

From this you see that verbs and their endings change in English too! (Does, do, speak, speaks).

If you want to go a little bit further, here is the whole present tense of the verbs **μιλάω** (to speak) and **Θέλω** (to want)

μιλάω	miláo	I speak
μιλάς	milás	you speak
μιλάει	milái	he/she speaks
μιλάμε	miláme	we speak
μιλάτε	miláte	you speak
μιλάνε	miláne	they speak

Greek	Pronunciation	English
θέλω	thélo	I want
θέλεις	thélis	you want
θέλει	théli	he/she wants
θέλουμε	théloume	we want
θέλετε	thélete	you want
θέλουν	théloun	they want

You will notice that in Greek it is not usually necessary to use the word for "I," "you," "he," "she," "they," and "it." This is because it is implied by the verb ending.

So you usually say
Μιλάω ελληνικά.
Miláo eliniká.
I speak Greek – instead of
Εγώ μιλάω ελληνικά.
Eghó miláo eliniká.
and
Έχετε λάδι;
Éhete ládhi?
Do you have olive oil? – instead of
Εσείς έχετε λάδι;
Esís éhete ládhi?

Adjectives

Endings of adjectives change depending on whether it refers to:
– a masculine, feminine or neuter word
– a singular or plural word.

Singular
η μοντέρνα εκκλησία
i modérna eklisía
the modern church
ο μοντέρνος σταθμός
o modérnos stathmós
the modern station
το μοντέρνο μουσείο
to modérno mousío
the modern museum

Plural
τα κίτρινα μήλα
ta kítrina míla
yellow apples
Τα μήλα είναι κίτρινα
Ta míla íne kítrina
The apples are yellow.
κόκκινες πιπεριές
kókines piperiés
red peppers
Οι πιπεριές είναι κόκκινες.
I piperiés íne kókines.
The peppers are red.

Questions

To ask a question, simply use the same sentence and change the intonation of your voice. The difference will be clear not only from the intonation but also from the situation you are in, for example, you're not likely to be telling a vendor he has some apples!

The Greek question mark is like an English semicolon, eg
Πόσο θέλετε;
Póso thélete?
How much do you want?

Talking about possession

To talk about "my," "your," etc, use the following words, positioned after the noun:

"my" **μου mou**
"your"* **σου sou σας sas**
"his," "her," "its"
του, της, του
tou, tis, tou
"our" **μας mas**
"their" **τους tous**

* For the different meanings of "You" see the explanation The word for "You" above:
"my"
το ρολόι μου
to rolói mou
my watch

"his"
το ρολόι του, της, του
to rolói tou, tis, tou
his, her, its watch

This and these

Like the articles "a" and "the," these words change according to the word they refer to.

αυτή η φούστα
aftí i foústa
this skirt
αυτές οι φούστες
aftés i foústes
these skirts

αυτός ο κατάλογος
aftós o katáloghos
this menu
αυτοί οι κατάλογοι
afti i katáloyi
these menus

αυτό το καρπούζι
aftó to karoúzi
this water melon
αυτά τα καρπούζια
aftá ta karpoúzia
these water melons

Things you like

The way you say what you like in Greek is very different from English.
Μ'αρέσει (M'arési) and **Μ'αρέσουν (M' arésoun)**.

Μ'αρέσει το κόκκινο κρασί, δε μ'αρέσει το άσπρο κρασί.
M' arési to kókino krasí, dhe m' arési to áspro krasí.
I like red wine, I don't like white wine.
Μ'αρέσουν οι αγκινάρες, δε μ'αρέσουν οι μελιτζάνες.
M' arésoun i aginares, dhe m' arésoun i melidzánes.
I like artichokes, I don't like eggplant.

What you are actually saying is "Red wine pleases me. Artichokes please me." That's why it's **αρέσει** (pleases) in one case, and **αρέσουν** (please) in the other.

Negatives

In most cases, negatives are formed by placing **δεν** before the verb. Sometimes the **ν** disappears depending on the letter the verb starts with.

Δεν μιλάω ελληνικά.
Dhen miláo eliniká.
I don't speak Greek.

Δε θέλω . . .
Dhe thélo . . .
I don't want . . .

Endings

Greek is a highly inflected language, which means that the endings of nouns, adjectives, pronouns, etc. have many different forms. However, if you concentrate on the stem of the word, you will still be able to understand the meaning of it, eg:

καταλόγος, κατάλογο, καταλόγου
menu
καταλόγοι, καταλόγους, καταλόγων
menus

Answers

Bare necessities

1 600 drachmas 2 27,500 drachmas, your passport

Questions and answers
a 3 b 1 c 2

Summing up
1 τρία και τέσσερα και εννιά ισον δεκαέξι.
2 δέκα και δεκαοχτώ ίδον είκοσι οχιώ.
3 είκοσι δύο και τριόντα πέντε ίσον πενήντα εφτά.
4 πενήντα έξι και εξήντα πέντε ίσον εκατόν είκοσι ένα.
5 σαράντα εννιά και εκατόν ένα ίσον εκατόν πενήντα.

Time tells
1 είναι οχτώ και μισή
2 είναι πέντε και τέταρτο
3 είναι είκοσι και είκοσι
4 είναι δεκατέσσερεις και δέκα

As if you were there
- Συγνώμη. Καλημέρα.
- Πού είναι η πιο κοντινή τράπεζα;
- Ευχαριστώ. Γειό σας.

Getting around

1 left 2 true 3 yes, 6000 drachmas 4 3000 drachmas first class by boat/5000 drachmas by hydrofoil, one hour by hydrofoil, 3 hours by boat 5 8am, 2pm 6 18,000 drachmas

Crossed lines
1d 2e 3b 4a 5c

Crossword puzzle
Down 1 επιστροφή
3 ποδήλατο 5 ίσια
Across 2 δίπλωμα 4 σταθμός
6 πού 7 μακριά

As if you were there
- Τί ώρα φεύγει το τρένο για Πύργο;
- Πόση ώρα κάνει, για Πύργο;
- Πρέπει ν'αλλάξω;
- Θέλω δύο εισιτήρια με επιστροφή για Πύργο, παρακαλώ.

Somewhere to stay

1 6000 drachmas, no
2 true, false 3 false, false
4 at 6am 5 Loutra

Match them up
1f 2c 3c 4a 5d 6b

Jumbled conversation
- Καλημέρα σας.
- Έχω κλείσει ένα μονόκλινο.
- Τό όνομά σας παρακαλώ.
- Τζον Σμιθ.
- Ορίστε!
- Το διαβατήριο σας παρακαλώ.
- Συμπληρώστε αυτό το έντυπο!

As if you were there
- Γειά σας, έχετε δίκλινο δωμάτιο;
- Ναι, πόσο κοστίζει τη βραδιά;
- Για δυο βραδιές, παρακαλώ.

Buying things

1 1200 drachmas 2 yes 3 no

Jumbled conversation
- Μία Αγγλική εφημερίδα παρακαλώ.
- Ορίστε. Τίποτα άλλο;
- Πόσο κάνει ένα πακέτο τσιγάρα;
- Πεντακόσες δραχμές παρακαλώ.

ANSWERS

Something missing
1 τυρί 2 γιαούρτια 3 ζαμπόν
4 ψωμιά 5 πεπόνι 6 ντομάτες

As if you were there
- Διακόσια πενήντα γραμμάρια τυρί, διακόσια γραμμάρια ζαμπόν και ταραμοσαλάτα παρακαλώ.
- Λίγο ακόμα.
- Τρία λεμόνια και μια σοκολάτα παρακαλώ. Αυτά ευχαριστώ.
- Ορίστε.
- Γεία σου.

Café life

1 no 2 false 3 2000 drachmas

Know your drinks
a φραπέ, γρανίτα, χυμό πορτοκάλι.
b καφές, τσάι, καπουτσίνο, ροφήματα.
c ούζο, κρασί κόκκινο, τζιν, μπύρα.

Jumbled conversation
- Χαίρετε. Τι μπύρα έχετε.
- Κορόνα και Αμστελ.
- Τρία μπουκάλια Αμστελ παρακαλώ.
- Ορίστε. Τίποτα άλλο.
- Ούζο με πάγο.

As if you were there
- Τι γλυκά έχετε;
- Έχετε γρανίτα;
- Μιά σοκολατίνα και μιά πορτοκαλάδα, παρακαλώ.

Eating out

1 baked, stuffed eggplant
2 yes 3 true 4 Would you like anything else? 5 yes

Fill in the blanks
1d 2c 3e 4f 5a 6b

As if you were there
- Καλησπέρα. Μου φέρνετε μια ταραμοσαλάτα, μια μερίδα πατάτες τηγανητές, φέτα, μια σαλάτα και μια μπριζόλα, παρακαλώ.
- Ένα μπουκάλι κόκκινο κρασί.
- Ένα μπουκάλι άσπρο κρασί.

Entertainment and leisure

1 midday, at the ticket office
2 Wednesday, 2000 drachmas
3 at 4 o'clock

Jumbled words
1 πινακοθήκη 2 θέατρο
3 παραλία 4 πισίνα 5 ντίσκο

As if you were there
- Τι ώρα αρχίζει το κέντρο;
- Τι ώρα αρχίζει το πρόγραμμα;
- Χρειάζονται εισιτήρια;
- Ευχαριστώ.

Emergencies

1 three times a day
2 fill in a form 3 false

Making connections
τσάντα handbag, βαλίτσα suitcase, πορτοφόλι wallet, διαβατήριο passport, μηχανή camera, λεφτά money

As if you were there
- Καλημέρα.
- Έχετε κάτι για έγκαυμα από τον ήλιο;
- Και γαλάκτωμα μετά τον ήλιο;
- Πόσο κάνει αυτό; όλα μαζί;

Dictionary

αγγούρι, το agoúri cucumber
αγκώνας, ο agónas elbow
αγορά, η aghorá market
αγοράζω aghorázo I buy
αέρας, ο aéras air
αεροδρόμιο, το aerodhrómio airport
αεροπλάνο, το aeropláno plane
αίθουσα, η éthousa room
αιρ κοντίσιον air condition air conditioning
ακόμα akóma more
αλάβαστρο, το alávastro alabaster objects
αλάτι, το aláti salt
αλεύρι, το alévri flour
αλλάζω allázo change
αλλεργικό συνάχι alergikó sináhi hay fever
αλλεργικός, -ή, -ό alerghikós allergic
άλλος, -η, -ο állos, -i, -o other
αλοιφή, η alifí lotion
αμόλυβδη, η amólivdi unleaded
αναπνέω anapnéo breathe
αναχωρήσεις anahorísis departures
ανάψτε anápste switch on
αναψυκτικό, το anapsiktikó soft drink
Ανδρών andrón Men
ανθρακούχο, το anthrakoúho carbonated
ανοιχτός -ή, -ό anihtós, -í, ó open
αντιβιοτικό, το andiviotikó antibiotics
αντισταμινικό, το andistaminikó antihistamine
απέχει apéhi is far
απλά κοιτάω aplá kitáo I'm just looking
απλό apló one way
αποβάθρα, η apováthra platform
απορρυπαντικό, το aporipandikó laundry detergent
αποσμητικό, το aposmitikó deodorant
από apó from
απόδειξη, η apódhixi receipt
αποδυτήρια, τα apodhitíria locker rooms
αποχωρητήρια, τα apohoritíria restrooms
αρέσει (μου) arési (mou) I like
αριθμός κυκλοφορίας arithmós kikloforías license plate
αριθμός, ο arithmós number
αριστερά aristerá left
αρκετά arketá enough
άρρωστος, -η, -ο árostos ill
αρχαιότητες arheótites antiquities
αρχίζω arhízo begin
ασανσέρ asansér elevator
ασημικά asimiká silverware
ασθενοφόρο, το asthenofóro ambulance
ασπιρίνη, η aspiríni aspirin
άσπρος, -η, -ο áspros, -i, o white
αστράγαλος, ο astrághalos ankle
αστυνομία, η astinomía police
ασφάλεια, η asfália insurance
άτομο, το átomo person
αυγό, το avgó egg
αύριο ávrio tomorrow
αυτά aftá these
αυτί, το aftí ear
αυτοκίνητο, το aftokínito car
αυτός, -ή, -ό aftós, -í, -ó this
αφήνω afíno leave
αφίξεις afíxis arrivals
αχλάδι, το ahládhi pear
άψητος, -η, -ο ápsitos, -i, -o raw

βάζο, το vázo vase/jar
βάζω vázo I put
βαλίτσα, η valítsa suitcase
βγάζω vgházo to take out
βεβαίως venévos Yes, of course
βεράντα, η veránda terrace
βερύκκοκο, το veríkoko apricot
βιβλίο, το vivlío book
βιβλιοπωλείο, το vivliopolío bookstore
βίλλα, η víla villa
βοήθεια, η voíthia help

115

DICTIONARY

βοηθώ voithó to help
Βορράς, ο Vorás North
βράδυ, το /βραδιά, η vrádhi/vradhiá evening
βρεφική τροφή, η vrefikí trofí baby food
βρύση, η vrísi faucet

γάλα, το ghála milk
γαλακτοπωλείο, το ghalaktopolío dairy shop
γαλάκτωμα μετά τον ήλιο ghaláktoma metá ton ílio after-sun lotion
Γεια σας Yá sas hello/goodbye (pl)
Γεια σου Yá sou hello/goodbye (sing)
γεμάτος, -η, -ο yemátos full
γεμιστά yemistá stuffed
γεμίστε yemíste fill it up
γέφυρα, η yéfira bridge
γήπεδο τένις, το yípedo ténis tennis court
γήπεδο, το yípedo stadium
για ya for
γιατρός, ο yiatrós doctor
γιός, ο yiós son
γκαρνταρόμπα, η gardaróba cloakroom
γκρέιπ φρουτ, το grape fruit grapefruit
γκρίζος, -α, -ο grízos gray
γλυκό, το ghlikó cake, candy
γόνατο, το ghónato knee
γούνα, η ghoúna fur
γοφός, ο ghofós hip
γράμμα, το ghráma letter
γραμμάριο, το ghramário gram
γραμματόσημο, το ghramatósimo stamp
γυαλιά ηλίου yialiá ilíou sunglasses
γυμναστήριο, το yimnastírio fitness center
Γυναικών Yinekón Ladies
γιαούρτι, το yiaoúrti yogurt

δαγκώνω dhagóno I bite
δάκτυλο, το dháhtilo finger
δείχνω díhno I show

δεν dhen not
δεν καταλαβαίνω dhen katalavéno I don't understand
δεν ξέρω dhen xéro I don't know
δεν πειράζει dhen pirázi it doesn't matter
δεξιά dhexiá on the right
δεύτερος, -η, -ο défteros second
διαβατήριο, το dhiavatírio passport
διαβητικός, -η, -ο dhiavitikós diabetic
διακόσια dhiakósia 200
διάλειμμα, το dhiálima intermission
διαμερίσματα dhiamerísmata apartments
διάρροια, η diária diarrhea
διασκέδαση, η dhiaskédhasi entertainment
διεύθυνση, η dhiéfthinsi address
δίκλινο dhíklino double
δίνω dhíno I give
δίπλωμα, το dhíploma driver's license
δοκιμάζω dhokimázo I try
δόντι, το dhóndi tooth
δραχμή, η dhrahmí drachma
δρομολόγιο, το dhromológhio schedule
δρόμος, ο dhrómos street
δυσκοιλιότητα, η dhiskiliótita constipation
δυστυχώς dhistihós unfortunately
δω dho I see
δωμάτιο, το dhomátio room

εβδομάδα, η evdhomádha week
έγινε éghine happened
εγχείρηση, η eghírisi operation
εδώ edhó here
είναι íne is/are
εισιτήριο, το isitírio ticket
εκδοτήριο, το ekdhotírio ticket office
εκείνο, -η, -ο ekíno, i, o that
εκείνος, -η, -ο ekínos, -i, -o that
εκκλησία, η eklisía church
έκπτωση, η ékptosi concession
ελέγξτε elénxte check
ελεύθερος, -η, -ο eléftheros free

DICTIONARY

ελληνικά elinikά Greek (language)
εμπορικό κέντρο, το emborikó kéndro shopping center
εμφανίζω emfanízo I develop
εμφιαλωμένος, -η, -ο emfialoménos, i, o still
ένας/ ένα énas/ éna a, an/one
ενδιαφέρει endhiaféri interests
ενοικιάζονται enikiázonde to let
εντάξει endáxi OK
έντομο éndomo insect
έντυπο, το éndipo form
έξοδος, η éxodhos exit
εξωτερική γραμμή, η exoterikí ghramí outside number
εξωτερικός, -ή, -ό exoterikós, í, ó outer
επαναλαμβάνω epanalamváno repeat
επείγον epíghon urgent
επιβάρυνση, η epivárinsi extra charge
επιδόρπιο, το epidhórpio dessert
επικυρώστε epikiróste validate
επιστροφή, η epistrofí return
επόμενο epómeno next
έργο, το érgho movie/play
εστιατόριο, το estiatório restaurant
εσώρουχα esórouha underwear
εσωτερικός, -ή, -ό esoterikós, í, ó inner
έτοιμος, -η, -ο étimos ready
ευθεία efthía straight ahead
ευχαριστώ efharistó thank you
έχετε éhete you have/do you have?
έχω ého I have

ζακέτα, η zakéta jacket (women's)
ζαμπόν, το zambón ham
ζάχαρη, η záhari sugar
ζαχαροπλαστείο, το zaharoplastío cake shop
ζεστός, -ή, -ό zestós hot
ζυγός, -ή, -ό zighós even
ζώνη, η zóni belt

(η)μέρα, η (i)méra day

η i the (fem)
ή í or
ήλιος, ο ílios sun
ήσυχος, -η, -ο ísihos alone (idiom)

θα tha shall/will
θα ήθελα tha íthela I'd like
θαλάσσιο σκι, το thalásio ski water skis
θέατρο, το théatro theater
θέλω thélo I'd like/I want
θέση, η thési class
θυρίδα, η thirídha safety deposit box

ίδιος, -α, -ο ídhios, a, o same
ιππόδρομος, ο ipódhromos racetrack
Ιπτάμενο Δελφίνι, το Iptámeno Dhelfíni Flying Dolphin (hydrofoil)
ίσια ísia straight
ισόγειο, το isóghio first floor
ιστιοπλοΐα, η istioploía sailing
ιχθυοπωλείο, το ihthiopolío fish shop

καθαριστήρας, ο katharistíras windshield wiper
και ke and
καΐκι, το kaíki sailboat/dinghy
καιρός, ο kerós time
καίω kéo I burn
καλή όρεξη kalí órexi enjoy your meal
καλημέρα kaliméra good morning
καληνύχτα kaliníhta good night
καλησπέρα kalispéra good evening
καλοριφέρ kalorifér central heating
καλός, -ή, -ό kalós, í, ó good
κάλτσες, οι káltses socks
καλώ kaló call
κάμπιγκ, το camping campsite
καμπίνα, η kambína cabin
κανένας kanénas no one
κανονικά kanoniká for adults
κάνω káno I do
καπέλο, το kapélo hat

DICTIONARY

καπνίζω kapnízo smoke
κάποιος, -α, -ο kápios someone
κάποιος, -α, -ο kápios, a, o any
κάπου kápou somewhere
καράβι, το karávi boat
καραμέλες karaméles candy
καρδιά, η kardhiá heart
καρότα, τα karóta carrot
καρπούζι, το karpoúzi watermelon
κάρτα, η kárta postcard
κάρτες kártes postcards
κάστρο, το kástro castle
κατάλογος, ο katáloghos menu
κατάστημα νεωτερισμών katástima neoterismón clothing store
κατάστημα, το katástima shop
κάτι káti something/anything
καφέ kafé brown
καφές, ο kafés coffee
κεντρικός, -ή, -ό kendrikós central/main
κέντρο, το kéndro nightclub/center
κεραμικά, τα keramiká ceramics
κεράσι, το kerási cherry
κεφάλι, το kefáli head
κήπος, ο kípos garden
κιλό, το kiló kilo
κιμάς, ο kimás ground beef
κίτρινος, -η, -ο kítrinos, i, o yellow
κλειδαριά, η klidhariá lock
κλειδί, το klidhí key
κλείνω klíno reserve/close
κόβω kóvo I cut
κόκκαλο, το kókalo bone
κοκκινιστό, το kokinistó meat dish
κόκκινο, -η, -ο kókkino, i, o red
κολλιέ, το kolié necklace
κολοκύθι, το kolokíthi zucchini
κολώνια, η kolónia cologne
κομμωτήριο, το komotírio hair dresser
κομπολόι, οι komboloi worry beads
κονσέρβα, η konsérva can
κοντά kondá near
κόρη, η kóri daughter

κόσμημα, το kósmima jewelry
κοστίζει kostízi costs
κοτόπουλο, το kotópoulo chicken
κουβέρτα, η kouvérta blanket
κουκέτα, η koukéta berth
κουλουράκια koulourákia cookies
κουνηθώ kounithó I move
κουταλάκι, το koutaláki teaspoon
κουτάλι, το koutáli spoon
κρασί, το krasí wine
κρατάω kratáo keen/last
κρεβάτι, το kreváti bed, lounger
κρέμα, η kréma cream
κρεμμύδι, το kremídhi onion
κρέπα, η krépa pancake
κρύος, -α, -ο kríos cold
κύριος, ο kírios main

λαδερά, τα ladherá vegetarian dishes
λάδι, το ládhi oil
λάθος, το láthos mistake
λαιμός, ο lemós neck
λάμπα, η lámba lamp
λαμπατέρ, το lambatér standard lamp
λαστιχένια βάρκα, η lastihénia várka (rubber) dinghy
λάστιχο, το lástiho tire
λάχανο, το láhano cabbage
λέγομαι léghome my name is
λειτουργεί litourghí works
λεμονάδα, η lemonádha lemonade
λεμόνι, το lemóni lemon
λεπτό, το leptó minute
λεφτά leftá money
λεωφορείο, το leoforío bus
λίγο lígho a bit
λίγος, -η, -ο líghos little/a little
λιμάνι, το limáni port
λίρα, η líra pound
λίτρο, το lítro liter
λογαριασμός, ο loghariasmós bill

μαγαζί, το maghazí shop
μαγιό, το maghió bathing suit
μάθημα, το máthima lesson

DICTIONARY

μακριά makriá far
μάλιστα málista certainly/of course
μανάβικο, το manáviko produce shop
μανιτάρια, τα manitária mushrooms
μανταρίνι, το mandaríni tangerine
μαντήλι, το mandíli scarf, handkerchief
μαξιλάρι, το maxilári pillow
μαρμελάδα, η marmeládha jam
μαρούλι, το maroúli lettuce
μάτι, το máti eye
μαύρος, -η, -ο mávros black
μαχαίρι, το mahéri knife
με me with, from . . . till, by
μεγάλος meghálos adult
μεγάλος, -η, -ο meghálos, i, o big
μέλι, το méli honey
μελιτζάνα, η melidzána eggplant
μενού, το menú menu of the day
μένω méno I stay
μεσάνυχτα, τα mesánihta midnight
μεσημέρι, το mesiméri midday
μετά metá then/after
μετρητά metritá cash
μέτριος, -α, -ο métrios, a, o medium
μέτρο, το métro meter
μέχρι méhri as far as/until
μήλο, το mílo apple
μηχανή, η (φωτογραφική) mihaní (fotografikí) camera
μία mía a, an/one (fem)
μικρός, -ή, -ό mikrós small
μικρότερος, -η, -ο mikróteros, i, o smaller
μιλάω miláo I speak
μισός, -ή, -ό misós half
μισοτιμής misotimís half price
μονόκλινο, το monóklino single room
μονός, -ή, -ό mónos, i, o odd
μόνο móno only
μου mou mine/to me
μου δίνετε mou dhínete I'd like
μουσείο, το mousío museum
μπάλα, η bála ball

μπαλκόνι, το balkóni veranda
μπάμιες bámies okra
μπανάνα, η banána banana
μπάνιο, το bánio bathroom
μπαρ, το bar bar
μπάσκετ, το básket basketball
μπαστούνι, το bastoúni golf club
μπαταρία, η bataría battery
μπεζ bez beige
μπιζέλια, τα bizélia peas
μπισκότο, το biskóto cracker
μπλε blé blue
μπλουζάκι, το blouzáki T-shirt
μπολ, το bol bowl
μπορώ boró I may/I can
μπότα, η bóta boot
μπουκάλι, το boukáli bottle
μπριζόλα, η brizóla chop
μπρούτζινα, τα broúdzina brass
μπύρα, η bíra beer
μύτη, η míti nose

να na to
ναι ne yes
νάτος, -η, -ο nátos, i, o there it is
νερό, το neró water
νεφρό, το nefró kidney
νιπτήρας, ο niptíras washbasin
νοικιάζω nikiázo I rent
νομίζω nomízo I think
νοσοκομείο, το nosokomío hospital
νοσοκόμος, ο nosokómos nurse (m, f)
νοστιμότατος, -η, ο nostimótatos delicious
Νότος, ο Nótos South
νούμερο, το noúmero size/number
ντίσκο, η dísco disco
ντομάτα, η domáta tomatoes
ντόπιος, -α, -ο dópios, local
ντους, το doús shower

ξενάγηση, η xenaghisi tour
ξεναγός, ο/η xenaghós guide
ξενοδοχείο, το xenodhohío hotel
Ξενώνας Νεότητας, ο Xenónas Neótitas Youth Hostel
ξύδι, το xídhi vinegar
ξυπνάω xipnáo I wake up

119

DICTIONARY

οδηγός, ο/η odhighós guide (book)
οδοντόβουρτσα, η odhondóvourtsa toothbrush
οδοντογιατρός, ο/η odhondoyiatrós dentist
οδοντόπαστα, η odhondópasta toothpaste
οδός, η odhós street
όλα μαζί óla mazí altogether
ομπρέλλα, η obréla umbrella
όνομα, το ónoma name
ορειβασία, η orivasía climbing
ορίστε oríste here (you are/it is)/ pardon
όροφος, ο órofos floor
όχι óhi no

πάγος, ο pághos ice
παγωτό, το paghotó ice cream
παιδί, το pedhí child
παιδικό pedhikó for a child
παίζω pézo I play
πακέτο, το pakéto packet
παλτό, το paltó overcoat
πάνα, η pána diapers
πανσιόν, η pansión boardinghouse
πανσιόν με ημιδιατροφή, pansión me imidhiatrofí hotel plan with one meal included
παντελόνι, το pandelóni pants
παντοπωλείο, το pandopolío grocery store
παπούτσι, το papoútsi shoe
παραγγέλνω paragélno I order
παράθυρο, το paráthiro window
παρακαλώ parakaló please/ you're welcome/don't mention it
παραλία, η paralía beach
παρά pará to (time)
παρκάρω parkáro park
πάρκιγκ, το párkig parking lot
πάρκο, το párko park
πάρω/ παίρνω páro/ pérno take/dial
πάστα, η pásta pastry
πατάτες patátes potatoes
πατζούρι, το padzoúri shutter
πάω páo go
πέδιλα pédhila sandals

πεζόδρομος, ο pezódhromos pedestrian zone
πειράζει pirázi it matters
πεπόνι, το pepóni melon
περιέχει periéhi contains
περιλαμβάνεται perilamvánete is included
περιοδικό, το periodhikó magazine
περίπτερο, το períptero booth
περνάω pernáo I pass by
πετρέλαιο, το petréleo diesel
πετσέτα, η petséta towel, napkin
πιασμένος, -η, -ο piasménos taken
πιατάκι, το piatáki saucer
πιάτο, το piáto plate/course
πιάτσα ταξί, η plátsa taxí taxi stand
πινακοθήκη, η pinakothíki gallery
πίνω píno drink
πιο αργά pio arghá more slowly
πιο κάτω pio káto further on
πιο κοντινός, -ή, -ό pio kondinós closer
πιο λίγο pio lígho less
πιπέρι, το pipéri pepper
πιπεριά, η piperiá pepper
πιρούνι, το pirouni fork
πισίνα, η pisína swimming pool
πιστωτική κάρτα, η pistotikí kárta credit card
πλατεία, η platía square/stall
πλάτη, η pláti back
πλατφόρμα, η platfórma platform
πληροφορία, η plirofría information
πληρώνω plipóno pay
πλυντήριο, το plindírio laundry
ποδήλατο, το podhílato bike
πόδι, το pódhi foot
ποδόσφαιρο, το podhósfero soccer
ποιός, -ά, -ό piós who
πολύ καλά polí kalá very well
πολυθρόνα, η polithróna armchair
πολυκατάστημα, το polikatástima department store
πολύ polí very/a lot
πονάω ponáo I ache/hurt

120

DICTIONARY

πονόδοντος, ο ponódhondos toothache
πονοκέφαλος, ο ponokéfalos headache
πόρτα, η pórta door
πορτοκαλάδα, η portokaládha orange soda
πορτοκάλι, το portokáli orange
πορτοφόλι, το portofóli wallet/purse
πόση ώρα pósi óra how (far/long)
πόσο póso how much
πόσο έχει póso éhi how much is it?
πόσο κάνει póso káni how much is it?
πότε póte when?
ποτήρι, το potíri glass
που pou where
πουκάμισο, το poukámiso shirt
πουλόβερ, το poulóver sweater
πράσινος, -η, -ο prásinos green
πρέπει prépi I have to/must
πρόβλημα, το próvlima problem
πρόγραμμα, το próghrama program
προσωρινός, -ή, ο prosorinós temporary
προτεραιότητα, η protereótita priority
προφυλακτικό, το profilaktikó condom
πρόχειρο φαγητό, το próhiro faghitó snacks
πρωί, το proí morning
πρωϊνό, το proinó breakfast
πρώτος, -η, -ο prótos first
πυρετός, ο piretós fever
πυροτεχνήματα pirotehnímata fireworks
πως pos how
πως λέγεστε pos légheste what's your name?
πως σας φαίνεται pos sas fénete how do you like it?

ρακέτα, η rakéta racket/bat
ρέστα résta change
ρίγανη, η ríghani oregano
ρόδα, η ródha wheel

ροδάκινο, το rodhákino peach
ροζ roz pink
ρολό, το roló blind
ρουμ σέρβις, το roum sérvis room service
ρούχα roúha clothes

σακκάκι, το sakáki jacket
σακκουλάκι, το sakouláki sachet
σαλάτα, η saláta salad
σαμπουάν, το sambouán shampoo
σάντουιτς, ,το sándouits sandwich
σάουνα, η sáouna sauna
σαπούνι, το sapoúni soap
σας sas your (pl)
σε, σ' se, s' at, to, on
σελφ σέρβις, το self sérvis self-service
σεντόνι, το sendóni sheet
σερβιέτα, η serviéta sanitary napkin
σερφ, το serf surfboard
σέρφιγκ, το serfing surfing/windsurfing
σήμερα símera today
σίδερο, το sídhero iron
σινεμά, το sinemá movie theater
σιρόπι, το sirópi cough syrup
σκάλα, η skála stairs
σκάφος, το skáfos boat
σκέφτομαι (σκεφτώ) skéftome I think
σκηνή, η skiní tent
σκι, το ski skiing
σκόρδο, το skórdho garlic
σκουπιδοντεκές, ο skoupidhondekés trash can
σκούρος, -η, -ο skoúros dark
σκύλος, ο skílos dog
σοβαρός, -ή, -ό sovarós serious
σοκολάτα, η sokoláta chocolate
σορτς, το sorts shorts
σούπερ soúper five star
σούπερ μάρκετ, το soúper márket supermarket
σπανάκι, το spanáki spinach
σπάω spáo I break
σπεσιαλιτέ, η spesialité specialty

DICTIONARY

σπίρτα **spírta** matches
στάδιο, το **stádhio** stadium
στάθμευση, η **státhmefsi** parking
σταθμός, ο (λεωφορείων, τρένων) **stathmós (leoforíon, trénon)** station (bus, train)
στάση, η **stási** bus stop
σταφύλι, το **stafíli** grapes
στέλνω **stélno** I send
στήθος, το **stíthos** chest
στις **stis** in, on, at, to (f, pl)
στομάχι, το **stomáhi** stomach
στον, στην, στο **ston, stin, sto** at, to, on, in the (m, f, n)
στρίβω **strívo** turn
στυλό, το **stiló** pen
συγγνώμη **sighnómi** excuse me/I'm sorry/pardon
σύκο, το **síko** fig
συκώτι, το **sikóti** liver
συμπληρώνω **simbliróno** I fill in
συναυλία, η **sinavlía** concert
συνταγή, η **sindaghí** prescription
συνταξιούχος, ο **sindaxioúhos** senior citizen
συστήνω **sistíno** I recommend
σφράγισμα, το **sfrághisma** feeling
σχέδιο, το **shédhio** map, plan
σωσίβιο, το **sosívio** life jacket

τάβλι, το **távli** backgammon
ταμείο, το **tamío** register
ταμπλ ντοτ, το **tabl dot** set menu
ταξειδιωτική επιταγή, η **taxidhiotikí epitaghí** traveler's checks
ταξειδιωτικό πρακτορείο, το **taxidhiotikó praktorío** travel agency
ταξί, το **taxí** taxi
τείχη της πόλης **tíhi tis pólis** town walls
τελειώνω **telióno** finish
τελείωσε **telíose** we've run out
τέλος, το **télos** end
τζαμί, το **tzamí** mosque
τζιν, το **tzin** jeans
τηλεκάρτα, η **tilekárta** telephone card
τηλεόραση, η **tileórasi** television
τηλέφωνο, το **tiléfono** telephone

τηρήστε! **tiríste!** keep (rules)
τι **ti** what
τι κάνεις **ti kánis** how are you?
τιμόνι, το **timóni** steering wheel
τίποτ' άλλο **tipot' álo** anything else
τμήμα, το **tmíma** department/police station
τον, την, το **ton, tin, to** the
τουαλέτες **toualétes** restrooms
τραγούδι, το **traghoúdhi** song
τραπέζι, το **trapézi** table
τρένο, το **tréno** train
τρίκλινο, το **tríklino** triple room
τροχόσπιτο, το **trohóspito** camper
τσάι, το **tsái** tea
τσάντα, η **tsánda** bag
τσιγάρα **tsighára** cigarettes
τσιμπάω **tsimbáo** sting
τσίμπημα, το **tsímbima** sting
τσίχλα, η **tsíhla** chewing gum
τσουρέκι, το **tsouréki** sweet bread
τυρί, το **tirí** cheese

υγρό φακών επαφής, το **ighró fakón epafís** contact lens solution
υπάρχει, -ουν **ipárhi, -oun** there is/are
υπόγειο, το **ipóghio** basement
υπογράφω **ipoghráfo** sign
υπότιτλος, ο **ipótitlos** subtitle

φανάρι, το **fanári** light (traffic)
φαρμακείο, το **farmakío** pharmacy
φάρμακο, το **fármako** medicine
φασολάκια **fasolákia** green beans
φέρνω **férno** I bring
φέρυ, το **féri** ferry
φεστιβάλ, το **festivál** festival
φέτα, η **féta** slice/type of cheese
φεύγω **févgho** I leave
φθηνότερο **fthinótero** cheaper
φιλμ, το **film** film
φιλοδώρημα, το **filodhórima** tip
φλιτζάνι, το **flidzáni** cup

DICTIONARY

φοιτητής, ο fititís student
φόρος, ο fóros tax
φούρνος, ο foúrnos bakery
φούστα, η foústa shirt
φουστάνι, το foustáni dress
φράουλα, η fráoula strawberry
φρούτα froúta fruit
φρυγανιά, η frighaniá toast
φτάνω ftáno I arrive
φύλαξη αποσκευών, η filaxi aposkevón baggage check
φωνάζω fonázo call
φως, το fos light
φωτογραφία, η fotografía photograph

χαίρετε hérete hello/goodbye
χαίρω πολύ héro polí pleased to meet you
χάλασε hálase it broke down
χαλί, το halí carpet
χανζαπλάστ, το hanzaplást posters
χάνω háno loose
χάπι, το hápi pill
χάρτης, ο hártis map
χαρτί, το hartí paper
χαρτομάντηλα hartomándila tissues
χαρτοφύλακας, ο hartofílakas briefcase
χασάπικο, το hasápiko butcher
χέρι, το héri hand
χθες hthes yesterday
χίλια/ χιλιάδες, χιλ. hília/ hiliádhes, hil. 1000
χορτοφάγος, ο hortofághos vegetarian
χρειάζομαι hriázome I need
χρησιμοποιώ hrisimopió use
χρώμα, το hróma color
χωρίς horís without
χώρο, ο hóro juice

ψάρι, το psári fish
ψήνω psíno I cook
ψυγείο, το psighío radiator
ψωμί, το psomí bread

ώμος ómos shoulder
ωραίος, -α, -ο oréos nice
ώρα, η óra hour/time

Sounds Greek

The good thing about Greek pronunciation is that the written form and the spoken form of the language are very similar. Each letter is usually pronounced in the same way each time you see it.

The Alphabet

Throughout Greece and Cyprus the Greek alphabet is in use. The guide below shows each Greek character, its approximation in the roman alphabet, and a guide to pronunciation in English.

Some letters or combinations of letters have the same sound:

αι and **ε** both sound like "e"

o and **ω** sound like "o"

η, ι, υ, ει and **οι** all sound like "i"

A α a like "a" in "man"
πάστα (pásta)

Β β v like "v" in "van"
βούτυρο (noútiro)

Γ γ gh like "g" in "go"
γάλα (ghála)
or, like "y" in "yes" (before **ε e** and **ι i**)
για τρός (yiatrós)

Δ δ dh like "th" in "that"
δεν (then)

Ε ε e like "e" in "pen"
εφτά (eftá)

Ζ ζ z like "z" in "zoo"
ζάχαρη (záhari)

Η η i like "ee" in "meet" (clipped short)
Κρήτη (Kríti)

Θ θ th like "th" in "thin"
θέατρο (théatro)

Ι ι i like "ee" in "meet" (clipped short)
τυρί (tyrí)

Κ κ k like "c" in "can"
καλημέρ (kaliméra)

Λ λ l like "l" in "line"
λεμόνι (lemóni)

Μ μ m like "m" in "mat"
μαχαίρι (mahéri)

Ν ν n like "n" in "not"
νύχτ (nyhta)

Ξ ξ x like "x" in "box"
ξέρω (xéro)

Ο ο o like "o" in "hot"
νερό (neró)

Π π p like "p" in "pin"
παρετε (párete)

Ρ ρ r like "r" in "rum"
ρολόι (rolói)

Σ σ, ς s like "s" in "set"
σούπα (soúpa)
or, like "z" in "zoo" before **β, γ, δ, ζ, μ, ν, ρ** in the middle of a word
κόσμος (kósmos)
ς is used at the end of words

Τ τ t like "t" in "top"
τρένο (tréno)

Υ υ y like "ee" in "meet" (clipped short)
υπάρχει (ypárhi)